"At Focus on the Family we often hear fron
with the realities of deployment, return to
relocation, and much more. I wish that all of
tis' excellent book, which is filled with pract.
of experience."

—Jim Daly, president of Focus on the Family

"Things break at the seams, particularly for military families in transition.
Tony and Penny Monetti provide urgently needed guidance and strong
encouragement as today's military families dip deeply into their wells of
courage. This book should be in the 'rucksack' of every military family as
they navigate and overcome the challenges of transition."

—Bob Dees, Major General, US Army, Retired

"The perfect companion for the military family in transition. Take a deep
breath, grab a cup of coffee, and sit down with the Monettis through their
inspirational yet down-to-earth book *Honored to Serve*. No matter where
you are in your military journey, you'll be touched by their humor, compassion, and grace-filled encouragement, and strengthened by their biblically sound wisdom and practical advice."

—Jocelyn Green, award-winning author of
Faith Deployed: Daily Encouragement for Military Wives

"A military family's ability to endure this transient and turbulent way
of life is rooted in mastering two skills: a creative resourcefulness and a
constant reliance on our unchanging Lord and Savior Jesus Christ. Penny
and Tony Monetti provide inspiring examples, memorable anecdotes, and
practical tools that equip readers to excel at both."

—Marshele Carter Waddell, speaker and author of
Hope for the Home Front

"Powerful! Practical! Personal! Tony and Penny Monetti know the difficulties and transitions of military life, and point you to the God who goes before you and stays with you in the battle for your marriage, your children, and your country. Learn from their experiences how to be a person of honor, integrity, and valor maintaining physical, mental, and spiritual balance. Every couple needs to arm themselves with *Honored to Serve* as their survival guide for military families in transition."

—Elaine W. Miller, speaker and author of *We All Married Idiots: Three Things You Will Never Change About Your Marriage and Ten Things You Can*

"*Honored to Serve* is an essential asset to help military families not just *survive* deployments, but *thrive* in the midst of service to their country. The Monettis' firsthand accounts provide practical advice needed to overcome military challenges and transform lives. It's a 'must read' for anyone who has signed up to defend their country, or pledged their love to that warrior."

—Vicky Hartzler, US Congresswoman, Missouri's 4th District

HONORED TO SERVE

Guidance and Encouragement for
Military Families in Transition

Lt. Col. Tony Monetti, USAF, Retired
& Penny Monetti

DISCOVERY HOUSE
P U B L I S H E R S®

Feeding the Soul with the Word of God

Honored to Serve: Guidance and Encouragement for Military Families in Transition

© 2013 by Tony Monetti and Penny Monetti

All rights reserved.

Discovery House is affiliated with RBC Ministries, Grand Rapids, Michigan.

Requests for permission to quote from this book should be directed to: Permissions Department, Discovery House Publishers, P.O. Box 3566, Grand Rapids, MI 49501, or contact us by e-mail at permissionsdept@dhp.org

All Scripture quotations, unless otherwise indicated, are taken from the Holy Bible, New International Version®, NIV®. Copyright ©1973, 1978, 1984, 2011 by Biblica, Inc.™ Used by permission of Zondervan. All rights reserved worldwide. www.zondervan.com.

Names and personal stories have been used with permission. To protect the privacy of individuals, some names have been changed.

Interior design by Melissa Elenbaas

ISBN 978-1-57293-757-4

Printed in the United States of America
First printing in 2013

To our beautiful children, Giuliano, Antonio, and Gabriella, who have sacrificed and served this country faithfully from numerous addresses, both stateside and overseas.

Thank you to our loving parents and encouraging family members; today's valiant warriors and their parents who raised heroes with a heart to serve; devoted military families who have honorably served; those who currently sacrifice from both the battlefront and home front; the dedicated patriots who will bravely enlist tomorrow, and the courageous families of our fallen heroes. We shall never forget their ultimate sacrifice.

We honor your valor.

Contents

• PART 3 •

Combat-Related Stress Care

• PART 4 •

Reintegration

• PART 5 •

Transition into the Civilian World

Acknowledgments

To all the men and women who answered America's call to serve, especially during wartime, including our son Antonio, we salute you. May God keep you embraced in His protective arms. To our mom, Joan Heriaud, for every prayer lap and daily nugget of die-hard encouragement you offered while we wrote this book, and for assuring us that the Enemy's attacks meant we must have been doing something right.

A special thanks to the beautiful couple who exposed their lives for others to see firsthand the challenges propagated by post-traumatic stress disorder and how they have demonstrated healing through helping other veterans.

General Bob Dees, you are our mentor, friend, and fellow comrade-in-arms. We value your experience, wisdom, and professionalism as you role model how to furrow the fields and create innovative programs to heal war's invisible wounds. Lynn Lowder, you are a true American hero, and we salute you. Your selfless service, stemming from your experiences as a marine Vietnam vet, to your current role of mentoring young veterans, is awe-inspiring; your contagious hope is changing lives. Delilah Nichols, we appreciate your true passion for our military veterans and the sweeping impact your motivation is causing in numerous educational institutions. Ken Schueller, your genuine heart to help individuals discover who they are so that they can achieve their career dreams and find life fulfillment is nothing short of amazing. Pastor Brian Classen, your spiritual guidance and warm friendship continually encourages us to "be the feet" of Christ. Kevin and Lani Ward, thanks for your friendship and relentless encouragement.

To our Discovery House team, your example of staying true to God's precepts sets the bar for other Christian publishing companies worldwide to emulate. We thank you for trusting God and giving us the opportunity to serve our warriors and their families through this book.

For us, there is no greater honor than to serve those serving this great country. It is our heartfelt prayer that God's strength and healing touch reaches the hearts of all those called to serve through books, ministries, research, websites, organizations, and prayers.

Introduction

You, my brothers and sisters, were called to be free. But do not use your freedom to indulge in the sinful nature; rather, serve one another in love.

Galatians 5:13,
NIV (1984)

In the last six seconds of the lives of marines Jordan Haerter and Jonathan Yale, they were put to the test at a makeshift barracks in Ramadi, Iraq. Should they jump from the path of the terrorist's oncoming truck that barreled directly toward them at breakneck speed, or should they stand fast and halt the suicide mission that could ultimately massacre the fifty unsuspecting, sleeping marines who lay behind the gate's entrance? In those last seconds, Lance Corporal Haerter and Corporal Yale made a life-or-death decision. They chose to honor duty, exemplifying the greatest act of love; they laid down their lives and saved their fellow warriors by firing their weapons at the truck, causing it to explode before it reached the barracks. The resulting explosion killed both marines but did not harm their fifty comrades in arms.

It is this rare valor that personifies the military warrior and family. It is honor to country, fellow warriors, and duty that protects America's greatest gift—freedom. This shared passion to protect freedom is why warriors and family members choose to live lives punctuated with uncertainty, including uprootings due to relocations and deployments, knowing that each worldly threat broadcast in the media may mean the end of life as they know it. It is this very passion to serve our country that compelled us to help military families overcome the unique challenges this extraordinary life presents and honor those serving: from the marine sweeping the desert floors for IEDs[1] to the army spouse sweeping spilled Cheerios from a kitchen floor in Fort Carson, Colorado. From the parents who release their child from their protective embrace into the uncertain arms of military life to the family members, friends, and America-loving citizens who pray daily, send care packages, offer jobs, and buy coffee for the warrior and family serving. *Honored to Serve* invites you to walk a day in the life of the soldier, marine, airman, sailor, or Coast Guard guardian and learn why your acts of kindness affect them so deeply.

We know. We've been there. In twenty-four years of military service, we deployed for war. We experienced the fear of combat against an enemy and mustered the courage to fight. We refit the family puzzle pieces when their shapes changed with each mission, deployment, and reassignment. We know the challenges a military child faces, such as attending six schools within six years, and sometimes even in another country. We have felt the heartache when

---

1. Improvised explosive devices, more commonly known as roadside bombs.

separating that child from his best friends and reassuring him he would make new ones.

As military parents, we have watched the son who as a little boy used to routinely dress as a GI Joe in oversized fatigues proudly march across the BCT[2] field as a new army soldier in a perfectly fitting uniform. Our prayers for God's protection over that child while he defends our nation have consumed many sleepless nights.

We have looked into the eyes of burn victims and disabled veterans and been amazed as they courageously help other wounded warriors. We have embraced grieving parents and spouses who choose to honor their fallen soldier's life by walking alongside others suffering similar pain. We have witnessed people of faith return from the combat zone, doubting God after witnessing war's atrocities, and we have watched wounded warriors' hearts heal when they turned their lives to that same God in question. We labored through marital fires fueled by communication challenges and military demands, where the only way to gain strength was to accept our weaknesses. We witnessed the spirited senior citizen lovingly greet and serve donuts and hot dogs to anxious warriors in airports, even on Christmas Day. We have ridden the financial roller coaster of retirement and post-military careers. We have watched overwhelming passions collide when two warriors from different military eras embrace; unspoken words convey what only veterans understand. We have reflected after serving our country over two decades, fully realizing how blessed we are to belong to the elite military family.

---

2. Basic Combat Training, also known as boot camp.

One certainty every warrior, spouse, military parent, or fatigue-loving friend knows is that military life is not for the weak-hearted. Transitions occur as frequently as the newest box-office hit movie is released.

What crossroads await you? A new assignment? Moving to a new location or country? Deployment to a combat zone? Reuniting with family? Loss of a loved one through death or a life change? College or civilian life? Retirement? While thousands of active duty, guard, and reserve warriors are deployed, many are returning to their homes, workplace, and college life. Many are trading in their fatigues for civvies. Some warriors harbor the invisible wounds of war and struggle to readjust to life "outside the wire."[3] Sadly, an average of eighteen veterans a day are committing suicide.[4] Many spouses who manned the captain's seat while their honey deployed now find themselves with extra responsibilities after the warrior's return because of medical disabilities, increased financial need, job loss due to budget cutbacks, or retirement. Often, these transitions test the strength of relationships between spouses, between family members, and even between the warrior and God.

You are not alone. We are with you. We walk this journey alongside you while you examine your direction, and possibly, redefine your life mission. We want to equip you with invaluable tools, give you advice from experts in their fields, and help provide wis-

---

3. A military term describing when a warrior serving in a combat zone travels outside his military installation's fence perimeter.
4. Rick Maze, "18 Veterans Commit Suicide Each Day," *Army Times*, Gannett Company, 22 Apr. 2010.

dom from above to guide you on your path. We will never leave a fallen comrade. We are here to help you heal from life's wounds, overcome current challenges, become keenly aware of the blessings military life provides, and guide you to a hopeful future. We honor the unsung heroes who have walked before us.

By the last page, you will discover that how you honor God, family, country, and your fellow man is the legacy you present as a gift to future warriors and families. You will ultimately know that the true, indwelling freedom that transcends life's circumstances results from trusting the one true Commander-in-Chief—our Lord and Savior.

PART 1

Families in Transition

ONE

Hop On the Ugly Brown Bus

Embracing Change

Be brave and strong! Don't be afraid of the nations on the other side of the Jordan. The Lord your God will always be at your side, and he will never abandon you.

Deuteronomy 31:6,
Contemporary English Version

"A bus? Really, Mom? We are moving our household goods from Illinois to Colorado in this . . . this . . . school bus?" At sixteen years of age, all I could think of was how embarrassing it would be to arrive at our new home in Loveland, Colorado, in a gargantuan, ugly brown school bus. What would people think? If anyone watched me step off that monstrosity, surely I would be friendless until graduation. As a self-centered teen, my mind focused on my own concerns. Never did I realize that my mom purchased the old school bus because we couldn't afford a U-Haul moving van. The

21

plan was that once we were settled in, my mom would resell it. In retrospect, I can see that purchasing the bus was a wise financial decision.

Both of my older sisters lived on their own at the time. One of them, my nineteen-year-old sister, Patti Jo, had earlier moved to Colorado. When my mom and I visited her, we fell in love with the majestic mountains and healthful atmosphere. My parents had divorced several years earlier, and my mom was ready to leave the past behind and move on. Moving to Colorado, near my sister, offered a fresh start. Moving also intermingled excitement with fear of the unknown, sadness of leaving good friends behind, and a hope of greater things to come.

As long as I could remember, my mom worked two jobs to pay the bills while raising three girls. After working eight hours as a high school secretary during the day, she would come home, change into her waitress uniform, and then take food orders all evening at a nearby steak house. As tired as she was on Sunday, she made sure we attended early church service before asking customers all day, "Do you want steak fries or a baked potato?" She saved her tips to help fund this move, sold our home (which didn't land much in a down market), and risked a new beginning.

I didn't realize in my sixteen-year-old brain the courage it took to relocate. All I knew was that I didn't want to be seen in this freshly painted brown monstrosity. (For all future school bus buyers, beware: By law, buses must be repainted a color other than school bus yellow when purchased for personal use.) If it weren't bad enough that I was nervous about relocating to a new school and making new friends, I was stuck riding in a monstrous contraption that would buzz down the highways of moving cars like an ugly brown vulture.

Thankfully, we crossed the Colorado border after dark and pulled into my sister's driveway unseen. I imagined sneaking through the backyards the next day, walking up to the bus, faking a confused look alongside other gathering spectators, and anonymously blending into the crowd. No one would know that the bus and I were related.

The next day, my relationship with the bus remained undetected. No crowd gathered as I had envisioned, but once we found a place to live, we would have to unload the household goods. Surely my bus affiliation would be exposed for all to see.

Within a week, we rented an affordable condo near the Rocky Mountain foothills. Moving D-Day arrived. As we began unloading the boxes, lamps, and bed headboards, a girl my age caught sight of the bus. I cringed as she wandered closer to watch the commotion. Surprisingly, she cheerfully introduced herself as Kellie. She had moved from Minnesota a month earlier. We would be attending the same high school. She invited us to her home to meet her parents, and then she asked me to her church's youth group meeting. This was the first youth group event I had ever attended.

Kellie and I became quick friends. The bus that I found horrendously embarrassing attracted her attention and lured her to meet me. After I settled into my new school, I made more friends and joined several clubs. My senior year I ran for class president—and won!

Looking back, I realize that it was my mom's courage to risk leaving everything familiar and embrace a difficult transition that instilled the confidence I possess today to overcome challenges. Her positive attitude rubbed off on me. It wasn't easy for my mom after moving. When life got tough, she could have U-turned back to Illinois, but she worked hard to find friends and make ends meet by cleaning people's homes by day and working at a restaurant at night. Her fortitude and work ethic landed her a human resources position in a major company that normally only hired employees with a college degree.

Military life has moved our family eleven times since I said "I do" to Tony. Eleven moves, I have discovered, isn't much compared to other military branches. Each time the orders appeared and I became apprehensive to leave my friends, home, and community, I remembered my mother's courage and that ugly brown bus. My mom's choice to bravely seek brighter horizons opened up many new opportunities, forged friendships (one which led me to experience a Christian youth group), and planted a seed of curiosity that would eventually bloom into my accepting Christ as my Savior years later. The move plopped me into the middle of God's country where I could explore and hike the breathtaking mountains on a whim. Had I resisted the move and refused to board that ugly bus, I would never have attended college in Colorado, met a handsome, young Air Force Academy cadet, and well, you know the rest. The brown bus was filled not only with household goods but also with a mother's inspirational courage and life's opportunities waiting to be unpacked!

You may see your next move, deployment, retirement, job, or school transition as a big, ugly brown bus, and you are reluctant to board. In fact, many military spouses demand to be dropped off at the corner and discontinue the ride. Although your next relocation or transition may appear unattractive, choose to optimistically jump on board. Your children will pick up on your positive vibes and be more likely to join with anticipation instead of rebellion. The ride may get bumpy in places, but depending on your outlook, it can be filled with great opportunities, unforgettable people, golden memories, and lifelong friends.

Dear Lord, transitioning to new surroundings is challenging. Please help me to see the good in opportunities camouflaged as an ugly brown bus and spread that optimism to my family. Thank You for all the friends military life has blessed me with and those I've yet to meet.

REFLECT BACK TO A BROWN BUS EXPERIENCE in your life when you were apprehensive or fearful. Describe your uncertainty. What did you do to reduce the anxiety? What blessings stemmed from the experience? What future brown bus opportunities await you? What actions can you engage in now to foster optimism and security for you and your family members?

Resources

Militarytownadvisor.com and Operation Military Family (OMF) can help with relocations and transitions. Learn more about these organizations in appendix C.

TWO

What's Your "Stealth"?

Identifying What Makes You Special

Each of you should use whatever gift you have received to serve others, as faithful stewards of God's grace in its various forms.

1 Peter 4:10

As one of the initial cadre of pilots chosen to fly the B-2 stealth bomber and after eighteen years in that program, I have gained a unique perspective on the power of stealth. Stealth provides the ability to penetrate enemy air defense systems undetected. The B-52, B-1, and B-2 bombers each carry large payloads of munitions over long distances and are designed to strike targets anywhere, anytime. But if I were asked to choose one of these bombers to take into combat, I would choose the B-2, for I understand the value of stealth.

Just as the B-2 stealth bomber has unique characteristics that make it effective, so does every person possess unique characteristics and talents. By better understanding your skills and harnessing that power, you can train yourself to achieve the results you desire. If you want to win wars, the daily wars that directly affect you, then it's best to use your "stealth"—your unique qualities.

It's with this perspective in mind that I challenge you to consider your "stealth." What makes you, you? Are you using your "stealth" to its maximum capability? If not, what's holding you back? Have you created a plan that identifies your one-of-a-kind qualities and points you toward achieving desired results? Are you using your talents to serve others? Many people are not asking themselves these important questions. Perhaps they feel they are too busy, so they decide to settle for the way things are. I'm here to encourage you not to settle.

A stealth bomber without its stealthiness is just another bomber. Similarly, when you don't use *your* unique talents, you become less relevant. God provides everyone with distinct characteristics. When you become aware of your gifts and use them to serve a higher calling, refining these attributes daily, it results in achieving genuine satisfaction in life.

One of the best ways to understand your "stealth" is through prayer. It's the first step in helping you see yourself as you truly are. By humbling yourself and admitting to God that you need His strength and clarity of purpose, you'll be able to harness the power of stealth, your unique skill set. If you need further help in discovering your gifts, ask your family and friends to help you. Have them list the top three gifts and passions they notice in you. Also, use online tools to help you assess your special characteristics and clarify your personality type.

On one of my B-2 combat missions, our aircraft went into enemy territory without any other aircraft supporting us. It was the first time the B-2 bomber was sent completely alone, thus relying exclusively on the power of stealth. When we checked in with the Command and Control agency near the theater of operations, we were told that the air war was cancelled due to poor weather and that we should return to base. However, we had been briefed prior to takeoff that we should press in alone, if required, as the targets were of vital importance.

So we did press on. I recall flying our B-2 Spirit above the weather at night and over enemy territory. Below us, the enemy was lurking, but because of our LO they were unaware of our presence.[5] After flying into a heavily defended area, we confirmed our targets and released our precision weapons. After our bombs struck the targets, our tactical display began depicting various threats. However, we exited enemy territory undetected. The enemy was reacting blindly to the impact of our actions but was unable to locate us. We successfully accomplished our mission and returned home safely.

After more than thirty hours of flying, I returned to my Missouri home in America's heartland, turned on the television, and witnessed reports about the targets recently struck by our aircraft (actually, the news reported erroneously that the attack had been accomplished by the Navy with missiles strikes). While I was watching the reports, Penny walked in and asked if I could cut the lawn. One minute, I was in combat halfway around the planet, and seemingly the next minute I was home watching my battle damage

5. LO is Low Observability, which is what makes the B-2 stealthy.

assessment on the news while being asked to do lawn work! Warfare has indeed changed over time. The value of stealth was verified that night. There is power in stealth.

The other half of your stealth is your character. If you're foolishly wasting time and energy in degrading your character, then your character will become your weakness. In time, it will destroy you. Unless you turn things around, you will lose opportunities to use your God-given skills. You see it every day. Illicit affairs, drug use, stealing, and the ultimate character destructor—lies.

Your stealth gives you power to take risks into uncharted territories and accomplish what others don't think possible. Sometimes you have to go at it alone to stand against insurmountable odds. I've witnessed individuals and their unshakable confidence that comes from understanding their stealth-like qualities. They are winners because they refine their stealth and know what they want to achieve. They have a plan. Conversely, I've seen people exposing themselves foolishly due to poor decisions and getting shot down.

Imagine flying the B-2 Spirit bomber into enemy territory with the landing gear down and lights on. Such reckless action defeats the purpose of stealth. Yet how many people do that daily? Why expose yourself to the Enemy unnecessarily? Instead, why not rely on the ability God has given you to get you through challenges and help you develop good character?

After landing from my combat mission, maintenance personnel checked the B-2 for any damage. If any blemishes were located, the maintenance crew would spend time restoring the surface so the aircraft could be sent into combat again. The same is true of our character. We will all have setbacks and do things we regret, resulting in flaws in our character. The key is to not give up but to have the will to go back to the ultimate LO technician—God—in order to be restored.

What's holding you back? Are there blemishes you're not proud of? You alone know the truth of these tough questions, but if you don't come to grips with these important issues, then you'll likely be destroyed. If instead you develop plans to locate character blemishes and consistently go to the ultimate LO mechanic for spiritual restoration, then you *will* be victorious.

It took me years to see what was holding me back. My defenses are up now, and I'm constantly working on maintaining the right stealth. I can easily fall back into old ways if left unchecked. But through careful self-reflection, discipline, daily prayer, mentoring from a few good men, and routine restoration, I improved my stealth characteristics and continue to be transformed.

If you've fallen short of maintaining your stealth—your unique, God-given skills and character—then be resilient. We all have setbacks. The key is to be tenacious. And never give up on stealth so you can take the fight to the Enemy. Stay in the Word of God and soak in the wisdom of this good Book. One of my favorite Bible passages is Ephesians 6:13–14: "Therefore put on the full armor of God, so that when the day of evil comes, you may be able to stand your ground, and after you have done everything, to stand. Stand firm then!" Don't forget that there's an adversary seeking to destroy truth with lies. Satan is real and should not be underestimated. Fight the Enemy, and remember that the end battle has already been decided. God wins!

The best way to right wrongs is be aware of your character and work daily to make it strong. There will be blemishes needing adjustment, but if you stay committed to your plan, you'll achieve victory. Stand up for truth and use your stealth to win. This war I speak of is not to be won with physical force but with a commitment to live a good life while serving others with your gifts.

As a B-2 stealth pilot, I developed a "flight plan" that helped me organize my personal goals toward achieving my life ambitions. If you want to develop and use a similar life plan (see chapter 4), it's vital to know your stealth and what you're most passionate about.

So what's your stealth? Are you using your stealth effectively to serve others? What is your life plan? Are you reading the Word of God daily? Are you at peace with yourself and God? If not, what is holding you back? Once you acknowledge what your stealth is and improve it daily, then you'll be able to live your dreams and make a positive difference in your family, community, and country.

Lord God, make me aware of my stealth-like qualities. Help me refine my skills and character so I can be strong in taking the fight to the Enemy.

ARE YOU AWARE OF YOUR "STEALTH"? Record your primary strengths and talents. What actions are you taking to improve your strengths? What are your weaknesses, and what is your plan to improve your stealth? Are you fighting the good fight?

Resources

Visit Kingdomality.com, Keirsey.com, spiritualgiftstest.com, and the University of Central Missouri's Focus program (www.ucmo .edu/gateway/focus.cfm) for personality profiles and employment tools that can help you see what you value, and identify strengths, weaknesses, and spiritual gifts.

THREE

Ohhh!

Building Self-Esteem in Children

But exhort one another every day, as long as it is called "today," that none of you may be hardened by the deceit-fulness of sin.

Hebrews 3:13,
English Standard Version

I waited for the "boos" and the "get off the stage" insults to hurl from the teens and those counting down the days to become teens who were cram-packed into the annual talent show at Kanakuk Christian Sports Kamp. (Yes, spelled with a "K.") Jordan, a thirteen-year-old, heavyset, acne-challenged girl, nervously hip-hopped across the wooden stage. She belted out her song like the elderly church lady who is completely oblivious to the fact that she sings off-key. I dreaded the sarcastic remarks that were about to be unleashed upon this unsuspecting young girl.

With clenched fists, I waited . . . and waited . . . and waited, but the expected insults never came. Instead, a group of energetic teens jumped to their feet as if the president of the United States had entered the room. They clapped their hands and danced to Jordan's offbeat song. Their contagious excitement spread rapidly until the entire auditorium rocked with loud cheers. Jordan leaned down to meet the crowd's welcoming, outstretched hands like an *American Idol* finalist. As she hit the last ear-splitting note, the crowd roared its approval. The young audience encircled their hands above their head in a circle to form the letter "O" while cheering, "Ohhhhhhh!" the ultimate compliment a Kanakuk performer can receive—a standing "O"-vation.

Tears trailed down my cheeks. But I was not sad. I had just witnessed an unbelievable act of kindness in the teenagers' "all about me" world. Before my very eyes, an insecure duckling transformed into a beautiful, confident swan—a 180-degree turn from the insecure girl who visited my nurse's office earlier that morning.

Even though this was Jordan's third year at kamp, homesickness prompted her to visit the nursing office earlier that morning; however, a call home to mom was not going to soothe this kamper's pain. Jordan's mother, Emma, had passed away three years earlier. While Emma was going through chemotherapy treatments when she was fighting cancer, she could have used Jordan's help. But Emma realized the importance of enriching her precious daughter's faith, so she made sure Jordan attended Kanakuk instead. And now, three years after Emma went home to the Lord, Jordan was still desperately struggling to climb from despair's dark pit.

The spirited kampers knew nothing of Jordan's loss as their loud, long-winded "Ohhhhhhs" ricocheted off the walls. Pity did not trigger their cheers during her nails-on-the-chalkboard performance. Jordan's peers were seeing her through the eyes of Christ: beautiful, full of life, and courageous. God embraced Jordan though the kampers' cheers—a trait demonstrated daily by the kamp's college-age counselors. These enthusiastic, high-energy young men and women model what it means to be "sold out" for the Lord, and they encourage the kampers to seek their approval from God, not their peers. It was hard to believe that just moments earlier an insecure, frightened young girl timidly stepped onto the stage. But now a vibrant star, who was excited to live life, stepped off that same stage accepted, loved, and worthy. Jordan's skyrocketing self-esteem radiated through the room. I struggled to swallow as I thanked God that my daughter was able to witness and participate in this esteem-building act of kindness during her teen years.

It is believed that a child's view of himself is cemented by the time he turns eight to ten years old.[6] Praising our children daily and providing esteem-building activities nourishes and grows the character seeds we lovingly plant during their early years, so they will be armed with confidence to overcome life's upcoming challenges. Military orders routinely catapult children into new schools and unfamiliar environments. Kids understandably want to fit in and often will jump into the first peer group that welcomes them. Many times, this peer group consists of high-risk kids searching to find

---

6. The Self Esteem Institute, "Questions and Answers about Low Self Esteem," http://theselfesteeminstitute.com/about-self-esteem.html.

acceptance themselves. Building self-esteem boosts confidence and helps transitioning children choose their new peer groups wisely. Reinforcing home-taught values through faith-growing events forms a strong foundational buttress to withstand the negative influences that bombard our children daily.

Christian parents' primary goals are to protect and raise children who love the Lord, others, and themselves. When children are young, they revere mom and dad, and usually accept their parents' teaching as truth. During adolescence, however, parents somehow lose superhero status. Seemingly overnight moms and dads mutate into blithering nincompoops. No siren warns us that an upcoming sucker-punch will whack us off our respected parenting pedestal. It just happens. Surrounding our teens with credible faith-growing opportunities outside the home (Christian camps, church youth groups, teen retreats, outings with positive friends, etc.) becomes a foundation upon which to build self-esteem, especially during the tumultuous teen years when peer approval is prominent.

Research suggests that the common denominator among those who have eating or anxiety disorders, depression, problems with drugs or alcohol, are part of a gang, are sexually promiscuous, cut, have issues with teen violence or bullying, or commit crimes is low self-esteem. Girls are particularly likely to be critical of themselves, and one-quarter of older girls reported that they did not like or hated themselves.[7] Forty percent of girls with low self-esteem compared

---

7. "What Are Some Low Self Esteem Statistics," *The Self Esteem Shop*, 2010, http://www.the-self-esteem-shop.com/low-self-esteem-statistics.html.

with eighteen percent of those with high self-esteem said they had experienced sex before ninth grade.[8]

Moving to a new school is normally daunting, but it can be down-right torture when an adolescent struggles to crack the friend code while simultaneously discovering hair in normally bare places. For the military child, who may change schools as often as batteries in a smoke alarm, smooth moving transitions depend on the child's esteem and the parents' attitude. My older son attended six different schools during middle and high school. During an overseas assignment, he attended school in one country while we lived in another. Although extremely difficult at times, moving transitioned into a positive experience. He became more outgoing, confident, and self-assured. My younger son, who wasn't a big fan of change, took more effort to become acclimated. My husband received plenty of speculating looks from fellow parents when he pried our reluctant son's gripping hands from the car door to introduce him to Troop 363's first Boy Scout meeting. Once the ice was broken, however, Antonio looked forward to each weekly den meeting as if they were offering him ice cream on a hot day. Each child is different, requiring innovative approaches to get him or her involved.

Boos, gossip, and insults will likely be hurled upon our children at some point in their lives. If we take the time to build them up while they are young, teach them to love God, and provide positive opportunities to grow their faith, they will be equipped to overcome life's imminent obstacles, even when they sing off-key.

---

8. "Self-Esteem & Sex: How Boys and Girls Differ," *The Self Esteem Institute*, http://www.theselfesteeminstitute.com/about-self-esteem.html.

As an African proverb says, "Where there is no enemy within, the enemies outside cannot hurt you."

Dear heavenly Father, please help my child transition through all the challenges that come along with military life. Help me find the faith-growing opportunities that fit my child's personality, reaffirm his or her value, and encourage a close relationship with You.

WHAT ACTIVITIES SPARK YOUR CHILD'S INTEREST? Are there any youth groups or Christian camps that offer these opportunities? In appendix C are numerous esteem-building resources and faith-growing organizations. If you cannot find compatible opportunities in your location, pray about hosting one in your own home.

Resources

See appendix C for organizations and resources to help children build self-esteem during deployments and transitions.

FOUR

GOTOT

Developing a Life Plan

Isaac planted crops in that land and the same year reaped a hundredfold, because the Lord blessed him.

Genesis 26:12

A bomber pilot's mission is to achieve Bombs on Target on Time (BOTOT). When our nation decides to unleash America's heavy air power against an enemy, it's the bomber force that makes it happen. Executing bombing missions requires intense training and preparation. B-2 stealth pilots train for six months learning the basics before learning about threats, weapons, and targets. After months of academic study, we progress to practicing landings and aerial refueling in full-motion simulators and afterward real time in the aircraft. Flying ten feet away from an air-refueling aircraft at night takes great skill and confidence. And lots of practice.

After learning the basics, we begin focusing on understanding targets. Once we've identified targets, we start asking the right questions to achieve mission success. Our ultimate purpose as bomber pilots is placing the right weapon on the right target to achieve a desired effect. We are focused. The mission defines our purpose and training. We are also disciplined. Planning is the key. It's not like Hollywood, which portrays pilots jumping into jets and making it up "on the fly." Very much to the contrary, stealth pilots spend lots of time planning to accomplish the mission.

Of course, most people don't fly stealth bombers. But we all have other important missions in life. Perhaps we can change BOTOT to GOTOT, Goals on Target on Time.

To ensure a successful personal mission, I reference my personal "life flight plan," which includes my plans and goals for balance in three areas: spiritual, mental, and physical. Plans include specific, measurable goals to be accomplished by a given time. Knowing what your mission is and how to clearly identify your target is a challenge, for I have noticed that many people don't plan ahead. If you're preparing for transitions, it is important to know where you're going so you can make your life mission happen with the desired effect.

By taking time to figure out your purpose, you can prioritize your efforts and develop a successful life plan. Not doing so would be like a B-2 stealth bomber flying into enemy territory without any weapons or assigned targets. Imagine how reckless and crazy that would be! Many people don't stop and think about what they want out of life. And that's plain old sad. If you don't know what your mission is, get ready for some stealth pilot training designed to help you better understand your mission. Similar to pilot training, it will be challenging and require sacrifice and discipline. But in the end, you'll live with renewed vigor and direction.

What I have found extremely useful as I begin to identify my life's direction is to get away. And I mean *away* for a few days. A dear friend, Lt. Col. Tom Fitzpatrick (USAF, Ret.) highly recommended that I attend a retreat to help me gain clarity as I was approaching a significant transition. After twenty-plus years of service, I was about to retire, and I was unsure what I wanted to do next with my life. It was a stressful time because I had to balance what I wanted to do and what I had to do. Perhaps you can relate. I was on the verge of making important career decisions that would affect my family, and Tom suggested I get away and attend what is called a "silent retreat."

For three days, retreat participants refrained from conversation except during mealtime. No television, radio, or cell phones. Just you, the Bible, and a few optional church services. During my three days, I listened to sermons from biblical scholars who clearly possessed a deep understanding of the Scriptures. I spent time in the Word of God, but mostly I was alone in prayer and self-reflection. On the last day, while walking along the Missouri River with a cup of coffee in hand, I found a spot that provided a scenic view of the river and valley below. While sitting there, I prayed to God while emptying the coffee onto the ground and asking God to fill my cup. I began writing on the plastic foam cup key words and lessons learned during the retreat. "Loosen control. Keep it simple. Joy. Depend on grace. God doesn't think like us."

I gained a great perspective and inner peace during that retreat, and I strongly recommend this type of thing to anyone struggling with a big decision or life transition. Trying to make sense of where you are going sure isn't easy. But going to God in humble prayer and spending time thinking, without life's distractions, is liberating. After the silent retreat, I felt refreshed spiritually and had a better clarity of my purpose and ambition.

I know you might be thinking, *Tony, you just don't understand. I can't get away for three days.* Or *I don't have the money.* If you are struggling with a significant life change or big decision, then you can't afford *not* to get away for quality time to seek clarity. Make it a priority. Open your heart, mind, and soul to the Lord, and He will give you peace and begin opening doors. Those are the basics. It starts with God. As the Scripture says, "with God all things are possible" (Matthew 19:26). Once you know what your mission is, then you can clearly identify specific plans and goals.

Every morning I review these goals, and this fuels me to work harder still. To help me achieve my goals, I review pictures of my desired outcomes. By focusing daily on what I value and want to do with my life, I can then chart out a plan. Success happens with a purpose and great effort—not by accident. I run into so many people who have an entitlement mentality. They expect others, such as the government or churches, to help them achieve their life needs and ambitions. No one is going to make your dreams and goals happen but you, fueled with the blessings of God.

By including your family in goal planning, you'll be in touch with their desires and use your energies toward helping them achieve their dreams. To help your family achieve balanced lives, focus on three areas: spiritual, mental and physical. I call this tool SMP, but

Penny calls it PMS. She thinks that's funny for some reason (see chapter 10). This structure provides balance and prioritizes your efforts.

For each SMP category—spiritual, mental and physical—develop "SMART" goals that are **S**pecific, **M**easurable, **A**chievable, **R**easonable and completed in a given **T**ime period. Forecasting into the future isn't easy, but by thinking about it and coordinating, you clarify your direction. Give prior thought to your plans and use a calendar. Every six months, review the family's progress and update their goals. By developing a plan for what you value and wish to achieve, you'll live a fuller life. Once you determine your goals, it's necessary to remind yourself daily how you and your family will achieve your desired results—your GOTOT. Balance in these three categories—spiritual, mental, and physical—will help center your life.

Accomplishing goals doesn't just happen on its own. It requires hard work and determination. Spending quality time with God will allow you to rest on His direction to help guide you in choosing the right path toward success.

By emptying my cup and asking God to fill my soul with His love and wisdom, which instills peace-of-mind and clarity, I allow my life's direction to become clear. My inner desire is to be a servant-leader for my family and others. It starts there. Progressing to identify the target requires prior thought and planning. By knowing your mission and by developing a plan to train your body, mind, and spirit to accomplish the mission daily, you too will be successful in achieving Goals On Target On Time.

Heavenly Father, help me to identify my life's path. Provide me with Your direction. Just as You blessed Isaac, help my family to harvest what we planted.

HAVE YOU DEFINED YOUR PURPOSE? What is your mission? What are your family's goals? What steps are you taking to help achieve those goals?

Resources

Creating a life plan will allow you to stay on target daily. Below is a tool to organize your spiritual, mental, and phyiscal plans. First, identify your goals and be specific. For example, a specific goal is "I will read the Bible for twenty minutes each day after breakfast," while a general goal is to "grow spiritually." See the difference? Next figure out how to measure your goal, or how to know when you've accomplished it. Make sure the goal is both achievable and realistic, but don't set your sights too low. Finally, give yourself a deadline for the goal to ensure that you complete it.

Spiritual/Mental/Physical Target

Specific goal
Measurable
Achievable
Reasonable
Time period

In times of transition, you need to know certain truths about yourself. Complete your life plan by answering the following questions. Review your answers and your goals daily.

1. What do you know?
2. What do you think you know?
3. What do you need to know?
4. What are primary threats?

FIVE

Tune It Up Before It Breaks

Preparing Your Marriage for Separations

A prudent person foresees the danger and takes precautions. The simpleton goes blindly on and suffers the consequences.

Proverbs 27:12,
New Living Translation

"The oil's changed and the belts are replaced. Windshield wiper and transmission fluids are filled. Son, did you load the two coolers?" Tony asked.

"Got it, Dad," Antonio answered while chewing a bagel.

"Brie, did you grab the ham sandwiches from the fridge?"

Brie answered, "Yep. Got 'em, Daddy-o."

Tony continued his checklist, " Penny, do we have the flashlights, flares, first aid kit, coats, hats, candles, and lighter?"

"I've got the first three, but seriously, Tony, we're only driving an hour away, and it's 98 degrees. Do you really think we're going to hit a blizzard in July?"

Okay. Maybe I exaggerate (a little), but the fact is, my husband is a safety stickler when it comes to preparing for road trips. He assures that our car is tuned up and that we are prepared to withstand any possible hazards before each journey.

After a speaking presentation for a group of Fort Bliss spouses, I asked one battalion commander's wife, "What do you think is the biggest factor causing military divorces?" Her answer made perfect sense. She said, "If a couple has unresolved issues or communication struggles before the deployment, separation only intensifies them. Often, these relationships lack the foundation to withstand deployment challenges." The Pentagon has reported that the military divorce rate is the highest it has been in ten years. In 2011, there were over 30,000 divorces that involved a spouse serving in the military. Now more than ever, couples need to perform routine relational maintenance checks to safeguard their relationships.

Like preparing for a long road trip, couples need to "tune up" communication to not only withstand deployments, financial challenges, parenting, relocations, reintegrations, TDYs,[9] and retirement, but also to keep everyday relationships running smoothly. Otherwise, like a tiny rust spot spreads and deteriorates a car's frame over time, an unresolved communication problem will decay relationships.

So how do we check to see if our relationships are running at top performance? Take a peek under the communication hood. That's how! If our relational engines purr like a kitten and if we are open and honest, then we can successfully navigate around life's hazardous potholes when they appear on our path. However, if we

---

9. Temporary duty assignments.

don't consistently fuel our communication tanks and check our needs gauges, then our emotional fluids will run low, inviting future problems. Troubleshooting potential hazards before heading out on life's road trips can prevent relationships from overheating, breaking down, and even worse, crashing into a divorce. One way to avoid this collision is for spouses to learn to speak each other's love languages.

When stationed in Italy, we lived one-and-a-half hours from the closest American base. If I heard an English-speaking shopper at an Italian market, I would dash across the aisles, tipping over pasta displays and a few Italian shoppers in the process. (Just kidding. I never knocked over any pasta displays.) Seriously, I was determined to communicate in my native language. I knew enough Italian lingo to ask, "What aisle is the milk in?" or chitchat about the weather, but when speaking my native tongue, I comfortably converse about the deeper things in life. It's how I relate best to others.

In his book *The Five Love Languages,* author Gary Chapman describes how we communicate with our loved ones using five different love languages that vary for each person. One love language usually dominates the others, just as speaking English trumps my Italian, but you can still communicate through the others. Which language do you understand best?

- Physical Touch (holding hands, frequent hugs, a light kiss on the neck, intimacy)
- Receiving Gifts (anything that says, "I was thinking of you," from wildflowers picked by the roadside to an intimate gift like jewelry)

- Words of Affirmation (encouraging words, compliments, a note with tender thoughts)
- Acts of Service (taking the garbage out, a foot massage, breakfast in bed, volunteering)
- Quality Time Together (riding alongside your partner in the golf cart—even when you don't golf—a walk after dinner, daily alone time to talk)

Usually, individuals express their love to others in their first language, which might not be the way their honey communicates best. It makes sense. When choosing a gift for a new friend, do you purchase something that you like yourself, thinking your friend will equally enjoy it? Just because you have a fondness for gardening doesn't mean your friend will unwrap those monogrammed pruning shears with the same enthusiasm. Similarly, we relate best to our partners when we speak *their* primary love language instead of our own.

Tony's emotional Italian heritage is very different from my Lithuanian/German upbringing. My mom never witnessed her stoic mother crying once while growing up, even when my grandfather, whom my grandmother dearly loved, went home to the Lord. A life mission of mine was to hear my grandmother say, "I love you," even though her actions spoke her love in volumes. I asked her why she never verbally returned my sentiments. She replied, "That's just not the way I grew up," and that was the end of the conversation.

Family members in Tony's Latin bloodline, on the other hand, display their emotions like a peacock spreading its feathers. They hug, kiss, cry, yell, and sing in public. Because I was raised differently, I prefer to save affectionate expressions for alone time. Now that I know physical touch tops Tony's love language list, I can meet his needs better, even though touch ranks lower for me. When I grab his hand as we stroll down the Kansas City Plaza streets, kiss him at a restaurant, or cuddle closely while watching a movie, his heart soars. Tony is now sensitive to my love language: words of affirmation. He compliments me for pouring my heart into raising our children and our military ministry. He consistently expresses gratitude for family dinners, even if the recipe flops. Parenting, ministry, and cooking take effort. Because Tony appreciates my initiative, I feel valued and loved and want to please him in return. Are you getting the picture?

Learning and speaking your honey's love language daily assures your relationships run at top performance, so that one day when you wake up next to your snoring-louder-than-a-chainsaw, rotten-egg-breath, and more-hair-in-his-ears-than-on-his-head (eww!) husband, your heart will still overflow with love for him and vice versa (although an unexpected spa gift certificate may be in order).

Identifying your primary love language helps fulfill each other's needs, especially during separations. If time spent together tops your love language ladder, then time apart challenges you more than someone with gift giving as their native tongue. Find creative ways to speak your honey's love language while separated, and keep your communication engines tuned. One spouse shared, "I currently live in San Antonio; my husband is in Korea. We have gone eight months without touching one another, yet we still feel so in love! Every week we have date night. I rent a movie and pull a chair from the kitchen, place it in front of the TV. We Skype until the movie starts (during previews), then I turn the computer toward the TV on the chair and we watch a movie together. We usually make dinner/breakfast and eat too."

Amber's deployed husband, Jerry, has the love language of receiving gifts. Amber contacted a buddy stationed with Jerry. She sent numerous gifts and meaningful trinkets in a package to this buddy, who was directed to secretly give them to her husband whenever he seemed down. The gift immediately uplifted his spirits, and his loneliness void was filled in the love language he understands best.

Other ideas include reading a devotional and discussing it together. There are numerous great couple's devotionals on the market today. Several are listed in the resource section at the end of this book. Devotionals may not normally be a part of your daily routine, but reading them together (especially when you are apart) will bless your relationship tremendously.

Pray at a designated time. Even if you don't hear each other's words at the same time, the assurance that God does is comforting. Tony and I read a chapter of Proverbs each morning to correspond with the calendar day. If we are not physically together, we discuss it later or e-mail our thoughts about it to each other.

Conversely, abusing or neglecting primary love languages triggers relational breakdowns. Spiteful words deeply wound the spirit of one whose native tongue is words of affirmation. Holding back physical affection from a hug-loving honey is like physically starving that person, and he or she feels unloved. When Tony and I trudged through our marital fires, we veered separate ways instead of toward oneness, where we worked together to fulfill each other's needs.

When my first book, *Choose to Dance*, neared completion, I focused all my energy to make the deadline. Tony steered his attention toward retirement and running our family restaurant. Treasured morning coffee, prayer time, and daily conversation vanished. Weekly dates became nonexistent. Because we were not fulfilling each other's needs, hurtful words were spoken, emotional stabs were inflicted, intimacy was withheld, and relational damage resulted. The cycle continued until we decided to put a stick in the marital spokes by attending professional counseling.

Along with speaking each other's love language, another instrumental method to tune up relationships is to identify communication areas needing strengthening. Schedule time together to take the "Communication Tune-up for Couples" in appendix A. This resource is specifically designed to expose communication areas in need of strengthening. If your relationship is already heading south, professional counseling may be the engine oil that saves your relationship from permanent disrepair. Divorce is an unwanted result of such a breakdown. Divorce not only affects you as a couple but it also wounds all those who love you. The collateral damage can be devastating, and the fallout can affect your family for generations. Go the extra mile to get help. Focus on the Family's website (see appendix C) will help guide you to find a good marriage counselor in your area. If you ever fear for your or your children's safety, get help. See the resources at the end of this chapter.

If you sacrifice time now tuning up your relational engines, you'll prevent future breakdowns. The end-state for couples wise enough to strengthen communication includes a home that is built rich with love and a holy, fulfilling union that will be enjoyed the way God ultimately intended.

Heavenly Father, thank You for uniquely creating us. Help us strengthen our relationship before and during life's inevitable bumps.

WHAT SPECIFIC ACTIONS speak your spouse's love language? How can you show your partner daily that you value him or her? How do you plan to strengthen communication before, during, and after military separations?

Resources

See appendix A for a "Communication Tune-Up for Couples" questionnaire and appendix C for several marriage-strengthening resources. If you are in an abusive situation, get help from your installation's victim advocate—the Family Support Center or Family Advocacy Program will connect you. Or call Military OneSource at 1-800-342-9647, or the National Domestic Violence Hotline at 1-800-799-SAFE.

SIX

Rank in an Ashtray

Managing Your Finances

*The rich rule over the poor, and the borrower is slave to
the lender.*

Proverbs 22:7

"What do you think, Captain Monetti?" asked my commander. A
few minutes earlier a young airman was standing at attention while
hearing charges of writing multiple checks with insufficient funds
with the intent to deceive. The senior enlisted advisor, known as the
First Shirt, had just echoed the opinion of another officer that this
airman be stripped of his rank and relieved from active duty for his
intentional negligence and lack of integrity. The military's relationship with local communities was hampered because of this airman's
excessive bounced checks in various towns. His actions brought dis-
credit to our Air Force and squadron.

I disagreed and asked for leniency and suggested that the airman
be offered professional financial counseling and mentoring. The

commander decided to give me the opportunity to help this young man. The airman was ordered back into the office and after saluting and standing at attention, he received the judgment. The airman was assigned to my office under my direct supervision and confined to his quarters for a specified period of time. Within days, the airman and I appeared before a civilian judge at a local town, and I asked for the airman to be excused for his indiscretions. I provided the judge with a plan that included financial counseling and community service. The judge agreed, and the airman's charges were dropped.

Afterward, we attended basic budgeting classes together and met regularly with a trained financial planner who worked with Family Services. This trained professional helped the airman balance a checkbook, develop a budget, and create a debt reduction plan.

It was clear that this airman started off badly by incurring lots of debt immediately after enlisting by accepting numerous credit cards and by purchasing items that far exceeded his pay grade financial status. His military salary was soon unable to pay the credit card bills and other obligations, so he decided to write checks with insufficient funds. After a few weeks of training, it appeared that the airman was on the right track, and he returned to work with his team. Unfortunately, within months, he resorted to his old ways and started bouncing checks again while getting deeper into debt. Once again the young airman appeared before the commander and First Shirt, but this time the commander had an ashtray with a razor blade placed on the center of his desk.

The commander asked the airman if he had anything to say in his defense, but the young man remained silent. The commander asked that he strip his rank from his sleeves with the razor blade and then place it in the ashtray. A new judgment was rendered, and the airman was punished with a discharge, forfeiture of all pay and allowances, and confinement to military prison. I was amazed that a commander could have so much authority, and the turn of events saddened me. It was my hope that we could help the airmen change his ways, but it was not to be. This eye-opening experience taught me the challenges that many of our warriors face.

The majority of our military is comprised of young recruits, and our enlisted troops do not make much money. Couple low wages with poor financial choices due to a lack of fiscal education, and you are destined to have problems. Many warriors are unaware of financial planning basics and are taken advantage of by some financial institutions.

When I fought against combatant forces as a military pilot, I studied the enemy and researched their strengths and weaknesses. As a combat-trained aviator, I took the enemy very seriously and didn't expose my wingmen or me to unnecessary risks. Breaking down the threats made sense, and over time, I improved my situational awareness. I created a mental picture of enemy fighter aircraft and understood enemy radars and strategic air missiles designed to target and engage our aircraft. Going to war is somewhat simpler than some of the forces we battle daily that are trying to destroy us. In many cases, these hidden threats cause havoc in our families, and they can drain the fight out of us. One of the greatest threats our warriors face is financial mismanagement instigated by unfair financial practices by certain institutions. Another great threat is a lack of financial planning and education. The topic of finances is not a flashy one, but it's an ugly culprit that instigates many marriage problems, and it needs to be addressed head-on or it will cause problems. By becoming aware of the threats, you can better prepare for the challenges that lie before you and your family.

Some financial institutions take advantage of military warriors by offering low-interest loans immediately upon graduation. They make it easy to get loans since they know the warriors will have a steady paycheck to pay the bills. Should a new recruit get involved in such a loan, he or she will be saddled with high monthly payments that often cannot be repaid on a military salary. These kinds of loans seem to be predatory—meant to take advantage of young, naïve men and women. Do not fall for such tactics. Learn early in your career to live within your means. Some financial institutions pressure military families with refinancing options when it's not in the family's long-term financial interest to do so. Before considering such options, it is best to look at long-term plans rather than short-term gains of lower monthly payments. Other warriors are overloaded with credit card debt and are unable to make ends meet.

The person who is going to take care of your finances best is you. Think of this challenge as a campaign combat mission that requires you to plan ahead. You can achieve long-term victory by developing a workable financial plan. You may lose some battles along the way, but the war can be won. It requires discipline, a strategy, and planning. A solid starting point is to create a savings account with at least three months of your pay in reserves. Develop a budget based on your needs and wants. If you are burdened with debt, use your monies to pay off credit cards, from the smallest to the greatest. As you complete paying off a balance, add the monthly amount you were paying from that bill onto the next debt, and in time you'll see the debt disappear. It's a great feeling when you finally pay off debt. Keeping a few credit cards open without using them is wise so that your credit score improves but only if you are disciplined to avoid using them. Your credit score shows your financial strength, and when you pay off debt your scores improves.

A financial planner can help you establish long-range goals such as college savings or retirement planning. The big picture strategy is to eliminate debt, create a workable budget, and build a savings and investment plan that includes adequate insurance protection. Avoid spontaneously buying the discounted flat-screen TV if you don't have the cash in your account to pay if off. If you are getting ready to deploy or retire, slow the train down. Plan on the worst-case scenario when you retire, in case the job you have post-retirement disappears. It happened to me, and it has happened to many others, so be forewarned. Just a few months after my initial retirement, I walked into the kitchen for breakfast. While waiting for my toast to pop up, I logged onto my flight schedule for the commercial airline where I had just been hired. On the screen where I normally found my flight itinerary was the word *cancelled*. Within just three months, this promising, up-and-coming airline took a nosedive and declared bankruptcy.

The Scriptures are loaded with wisdom on how to grow financially stronger and how best to use your finances to help others.

The Bible encourages us to avoid debt and to be a cheerful giver. In 2 Corinthians 9:7, Paul says, "Each of you should give what you have decided in your heart to give, not reluctantly or under compulsion, for God loves a cheerful giver." Imagine having a strong financial portfolio and being able to donate to worthy causes. It can and will be done if you are wise and make good financial decisions. There are many worthy causes, and if you're in a financial position to do so, you can improve lives through your generosity. Those weighed down with debt are unable to help others, for they can barely help themselves, and thus are distracted from performing their mission. By being on the same page with your spouse and family, you too can achieve financial peace and prepare for the future. There are many military friendly financial institutions available to help you achieve financial success, such as USAA Federal Savings Bank and Navy Federal Credit Union.

If you are an entrepreneur and are interested in starting your own business, then do the homework. Be sure that you have a good product and know how to market it. Before starting your own business and investing monies, develop a realistic business plan. When working on my family business, I found a tremendous resource designed to help veterans develop plans and get strong mentoring advice from professionals who have a heart to help veterans. The Service Corp of Retired Executives (SCORE) organization is a nonprofit association designed to help veteran small businesses get off the ground and achieve financial goals (see score.org). This group offers mentors to develop business plans and marketing strategies. It also has workshops and online tools to help your business grow.

There are many tools available to help warriors prepare for their financial future, but the best one to make it happen is you. Standing with the young airman years ago in front of a commander's desk reminded me of the sad financial state of some our warriors when it comes to understanding finances and making fiscal decisions. Too many warriors are choosing the same fate as that airman. Although they may not be bouncing checks, they lack discipline and have no plan. They spend because they can and charge because of easy accessibility.

As the leader of your family, be the protector of your family's financial condition by developing wise plans for your family's future. Develop a balanced portfolio that has as its foundation savings, investments, and life insurance. By achieving your family's financial plans, you will be better able to give to others and to help your family achieve their dreams and aspirations. It just requires that warrior attitude, discipline, and focus. We need good warriors to stay in the fight and advance in rank rather than see their careers end up in an ashtray.

Give me wisdom to save my monies and the courage to do the right thing with my finances. Help me to be disciplined and a good steward of my treasures. Provide me with mentors to help me make wise financial decisions so we can better prepare for future challenges and opportunities.

ARE YOU IN CONTROL of your debt, or does it rule your life? What steps are you taking to eliminate debt? Have you met with various financial planners to help you create a financial portfolio to prepare your family for future goals?

Resources

See "Financial Planning" in appendix C for helpful books and websites.

PART 2

Deployments

SEVEN

Be REAL

Achieving Physical Balance

Whatever your hand finds to do, do it with all your might.
Ecclesiastes 9:10

Military warriors must perform under extreme conditions. There's nothing more uncomfortable than wearing a chemical warfare suit under the extreme heat conditions of the desert. Deployments and short-notice TDYs are commonplace in our profession, so you'll never know when you'll be called upon to operate under these extreme situations. Therefore, the time for preparation is now. Being physically fit builds not only physical strength but also inner power, which is essential for success. By pushing one's body to do what it intrinsically does not want to do, well, that's the stuff that describes courage.

After years of researching various diet and exercise programs and while experiencing other cultures around the world, I developed a fitness program resulting in a permanent, healthy lifestyle change. After being stationed in Italy for a couple of years, my family and I fell in love with the Italian way of life. I've taken the liberty of sharing some of my observations of this amazing culture that I've woven into my diet and fitness plans. This new lifestyle change focuses on desired results, leading to personal rewards and ultimately, good health. So are you ready to get "real" with yourself? Good.

REAL stands for **R**ewards, **E**at to Live, **A**ll-in during workouts, and **L**ive like an Italian. The quest to be **REAL** begins with rewarding yourself first.

Rewards. Most people want to know, "What's in it for me?" By starting with rewards, you'll be more inclined to exercise because you'll ultimately be the beneficiary of your actions. When creating rewards, start with realistic expectations and plans to make your goals achievable. One caveat: set weight and fitness standards one level less than the ideal. It takes time getting your body, mind, and emotions excited about working out. In fact, it takes about one month to get into a rhythm where the body actually builds up enough endorphins to fire you up. Avoid extremes. Losing more than 10 percent of your weight in a few weeks is not healthy. Determine what weight and waist size you wish to achieve and develop a timetable for reaching those goals. Write it all down, and track your progress. Once the program has been completed, reward yourself. Visualizing goals is the key to achieving them. Daily, review pictures of your desired end results and your set rewards. Reference your life plan (see chapters 2 and 4). The rewards could be attending an exciting NASCAR race, spending a relaxing day fishing, or buying new clothes. Make your reward a priority in order to have family fun as well as you work toward common goals.

Family is a huge part of Italian heritage, and while stationed in Italy, I experienced and embraced the Italian culture wholeheartedly. Italians value God, family, soccer, arts, and music—and not necessarily in that order. Perhaps a future reward could be for you and your family to take a hop, or a space "A" available flight, and visit "Bella Italia" to see for yourself what the hype is all about. Be sure to visit Florence, Venice, and Rome. Did I mention that Italians know how to eat and that their pizza is *fantastico*?

Eat to live. When living in Italy, I noticed stark differences between Americans and Italians. It was rare to find overweight Italians, whereas in America over one third of adults and 17 percent of youth are obese.[10] The common saying that you should "eat to live and not live to eat" is true. Italians are known for eating balanced meals that include healthy ingredients. They shy away from fatty, greasy fast foods. I traveled to most of their cities and never saw an "all you can eat" buffet. You'll find Italians enjoying their foods in the market square as they search for the ripest fruits and brightest vegetables. They love their pastas, but they consume small plate sizes and don't overeat.

The actual times they eat make no sense, but it works for them. I recall that on our first day in Italy we couldn't find a restaurant open at six p.m. for dinner. That's because Italian restaurants open at eight.

---

10. Cynthia L. Ogden, Margaret D. Carroll, Brian K. Kit, and Katherine M. Flegal, "Prevalence of Obesity in the United States 2009–2010," *NCHS Data Brief* 82 (2012).

Imagine that, eating a meal right before bedtime. Again, it makes no sense, yet most Italians are trim. They drink several espressos during the day, have a glass of wine with the evening meal, and drink lots of water. Italians include olive oil and balsamic vinegar in the preparation of foods and enjoy fresh seafood, and they prefer lean meat to red meat.

Another eye-opening observation during my two years in Italy was that I never saw one drunken Italian. It's against their culture to overindulge in alcoholic beverages, and they find it strange when Americans drink to excess. My family and I were amazed that an average Italian family spends an hour or two together during their main meals. They space out the healthy appetizers, small pasta dishes, grilled fish or lean meats, salads, and fresh fruit to enjoy the fellowship with one another. They'll usually have a light dessert with an espresso, and perhaps savor an after-dinner drink to aid with digestion, or so they say. Interested in losing weight? The Italian plan is simple. Watch what you put in your mouth. Eat healthy and don't overindulge.

There are numerous dieting programs, and it's best that you find one that works for you. Some people eat only fruits and vegetables. Others follow a caveman diet. Have you heard of the Eskimo diet? I prefer to eat like an Italian—one who values balanced meals of all food groups. Once you figure out a diet plan that works for you, develop a fitness program to meet your needs. Schedule the time to work it out, or it won't happen.

All-in during workouts. Work out in the mornings. Most people typically have more energy in the morning and afterward feel stronger throughout the day. There's clear evidence indicating that elevating your heart rate before bedtime is not beneficial to your circadian rhythm and could lead to poor sleep. There are many fitness and community centers available to meet your exercise needs. I invested in quality workout equipment and home workout programs. Consider it an investment in your future.

"Do your best and forget the rest" is a famous saying of nationally recognized fitness trainer Tony Horton. Tony is the creator of P90X—a unique home fitness program with proven results. Each time I struggled to do another push-up, his motivating words inspired me to try one more. It takes discipline to perform physical fitness for 30–45 minutes, but in time that discipline becomes a habit and eventually morphs itself into a positive lifestyle change. When exercising, put your workout clothes on and alternate days between cardio and weight lifting. Plan to break a sweat. Don't work out in your pajamas or a make it a socializing event.

When exercising with free weights, it's best to perform three sets of eight to twelve repetitions, using weights that culminate in the last repetition producing a slight burn in your muscles. You literally need to build new muscle, so that slight burn is good. In time, you'll reduce fat and replace it with muscle. Don't be discouraged if you first gain weight. Muscle weighs more than fat. Stay committed to success, and have a can-do attitude. If your desire is to tone your body, then it's best doing more repetitions with less weight. Want to look like the Hulk? Then perform fewer reps with more weight. Since it takes about thirty days to form a new habit, stick with it. Lifting weights and doing yoga-type exercises allow for strength *and* balance. By alternating these activities, you'll be amazed at how your shape changes. There's overwhelming evidence that vigorous exercise relieves stress, conditions the heart, and decreases depression.

One of the fascinating differences I noticed in Italy was that Italians ride their bikes or take family walks together called *una passeggiata* along the piazza. My 94-year-old grandfather biked daily to the *mercato* to purchase fresh fruits and vegetables. Each night he would stand before an open window and take in deep breaths, and then hold his breath in for a few seconds. He claimed that it was the key to his longevity. Italians enjoy outdoor activities such as biking, jogging, and tennis. Italians love sports, especially soccer. It's important that you consult a physician before getting into a rigorous exercise program. That said, be "all in" when working out.

Live like an Italian. During the first week in Italy, my Italian coworkers asked if I'd like to join them for some café. I explained that I had too much work to do. One of the officers replied while curling his fingers together and bobbing his hands up and down, "Raffaele," which is my first name (Antonio's my middle name), "Americans live to work, whereas we Italians, we work to live." The old adage, "When in Rome do as the Romans," suddenly came to mind, and I joined my fellow NATO officers for a café.

While in "Bella Italia" during our nightly *una passeggiata* by the piazza, people dressed elegantly while enjoying the amazing taste of *gelato* (ice cream like none other in the world). *Nocciola* was my favorite.

Their work ethic is completely different from ours. At first, I couldn't understand how they got anything done. They prefer face-to-face meetings rather than e-mailing each other while working in the same building. They literally take three to four coffee breaks per day. Taking numerous breaks didn't make sense at first, but it slowly became apparent that there was great social value, and the team seemed more in tune with themselves, their families, and their mission. I think the caffeine affects their metabolism too, for they seem fired up all the time.

We're unlikely to completely embrace the Italian culture in America, but maybe, just maybe, we can learn something from these amazing people. Commit to a lifestyle plan that works for you, and in time you'll have dependable results and feel healthy. Be **REAL**, and maybe a bit more Italian too, in the way you eat, play, and live. Try it. You just might like it! Be Italian.

God, I am tired of not living up to my expectations. Help me have the motivation and endurance to get up and do what I know is best for my body and me. Help me to be REAL as I strive toward a healthy lifestyle change.

ARE YOU COMMITTED TO BEING REAL with yourself? How many times a week do you work out? Are you "all in" during your workouts? In what areas can you improve? Have you established realistic weight and fitness goals? When was the last time you walked over to a coworker to ask how he or she was doing rather than shoot an e-mail to that person? What rewards can you set that will motivate you to be REAL?

EIGHT

We Will Get Our Jerseys Dirty

Standing Strong During Trials

*Do not be surprised at the painful trial you are suffering,
as though something strange were happening to you. But
rejoice that you participate in the sufferings of Christ, so
that you may be overjoyed when his glory is revealed.*

1 Peter 4:12–13,
NIV (1984)

Reading the "Welcome to the St. Luke's Cancer Institute" sign mentally smacked Tony, my daughter Brie, and me into stark reality as we stepped off the elevator onto the fifth floor. Welcome to the cancer ward? Are they actually glad we are here? We counted down the room numbers on the tan-colored doors of the patients' rooms until we came to 5130—my son's room. It was now sinking in. Antonio, my twenty-year-old army warrior, had been admitted as a patient into the cancer ward.

I had looked at my caller ID at 1:15 p.m. earlier that day. *Why is Antonio calling? He never calls during his Army Reserve monthly drill.* I answered and heard an anxious voice, "Mom, they let me go early. My lips turned black and are swollen. I need to see a doctor." *Black lips?* My mind searched through its cobwebs of allergic responses and other stored medical information. Black lips turned up nothing. He continued, "I'll meet you at the emergency room." *Emergency room?* I hadn't seen Antonio's lips, but this is the kid who won't even take Tylenol when his head pounds from a raging headache. For him to bypass home and drive directly to the ER meant his condition was serious.

I met Antonio at our small-town hospital. His black lips paired with military fatigues made him look like a "Goth" soldier. Red and black spots, the size of small freckles, covered his face. This was like no allergic reaction I had ever witnessed in my nursing experience. Even the medical personnel asked permission to photograph him since they had never seen these unusual symptoms before. The doctor's exam revealed the small red spots, called *petechiae*, covered his feet and legs, as well as his face. Blood tests flagged a life-threatening low platelet count, and he was hemorrhaging internally. I held back the petrified emotions that lurked beneath a calm facade.

Just the night before, Tony and I, along with several other proud parents, shot photos of our children dressed in their best suits and flowing, colorful gowns as we celebrated my daughter's first prom. Now, one day later, we found ourselves gathered around a hospital bed, praying that my son didn't have leukemia or another form of cancer. How life changes from one day to the next! God foreknew our impending storm that Sunday, and I believe, prepared our pastor with a message earlier that morning intended to arm Antonio (and us) with strength for the upcoming days. While we anxiously waited in our small town's ER for the doctor's diagnosis, I conveyed my personal interpretation of the pastor's message to Antonio:

"When Pastor Brian (little Brian at this point in the story) returned home from his youth football games, he'd strip off his game jersey and hand it to his mother. She would neatly replace the spotless shirt back on its hanger. No dirt or grass stained Brian's jersey like his teammates who had actually *played* in the game. Although Brian held a team position, he spent his early football days watching his fellow teammates from the sidelines until he was older. Pastor Brian's childhood experience can relate to our Christian walk and your being in this emergency room. Many of us own a *Christian* team uniform, but how do we handle life's tackles when we are thrown onto the field? Even though we may not like the position the coach has put us in, do we ask to be removed from the game and hang up our Christian jersey, or are we ready to reflect God's glory through our circumstances? How do we react when we feel the sting of life's tackles? How does our faith condition us through life's struggles to become wiser and strengthen us to successfully execute the next play?

"Often we Christians sit safely on life's sidelines as spectators when it comes to sharing the reason for our faith. We remain in our Christian circles, silent for fear of others' rejection. We stay passive and don't contest issues that require taking a godly stance. We avoid stepping onto the field, but life's circumstances, even like this illness, sometimes throw us onto that field even though we don't want to play. As Christians, our jerseys will get dirty. When the final seconds count down on life's time clock, and the moment arrives to hang up our earthly jerseys, they should be stained with a deepened faith from the challenges we've tackled victoriously. Antonio, right now the coach is pulling you from the sidelines and throwing you smack into the game. You are about to get your jersey dirty. Are you ready to tackle this?" Antonio's broad smile revealed that he was up for the challenge. Within minutes, Antonio was transported by ambulance to St. Luke's Cancer Institute in Kansas City.

For several days the specialists tested for leukemia and other cancers. Antonio courageously underwent each scan, x-ray, and test, absorbing the "worst-case scenarios" like a warrior completely armed for battle. His ironclad faith strengthened me as I walked the halls, waiting for test results. However, troublesome thoughts would weave their way into my mind. *What if he does have cancer? What if he has to suffer through chemotherapy? What if, God forbid, he goes home to the Lord before getting married and having children and experiencing all of life's wonderful opportunities? How do I deal with this?* Then I remembered. My jersey was gathering stains as well, and I surrendered my worry to God and prayed for His strength to carry me through.

Military life routinely throws warriors and their families onto the playing field. Warriors come face-to-face with their mortality as they deploy into dangerous territories. Home-front spouses and military parents carry an underlying fear that their warrior won't return, and if they do, will they return as the same person they were before leaving?

Antonio's ongoing health condition continues to test his faith, although we are thankful it is much less serious than what we first thought it to be. However, this is not always the outcome. As challenging deployments and transitions punctuate our military lives, living out faith demonstrates to others that not only are you on the Christian team, but that you also can claim victory during each challenging season with God-given strength. Even if you face Goliath-sized opponents and the field's condition is messy, when the time clock runs out, your jersey will be stained with the blessings that come from trusting the ultimate Coach.

Dear Lord, I'm often afraid to face life's tackles and don't want to be thrown onto the playing field. Arm me with Your strength and peace that transcends all understanding.

EXAMINE YOUR FAITH. Are you checking the Christian box that you're on the team, but you're still afraid to step onto the field? What can you do today to stain your jersey by leaving the comfort zone? This week? This year? How has life thrown you on the playing field in positions you would rather not play? How does trusting the Lord change the game field's conditions?

NINE

Losing My Cross to Find It

Taking Time to Pray

The blind receive sight, the lame walk, those who have leprosy are cleansed, the deaf hear, the dead are raised, and the good news is proclaimed to the poor.

Matthew 11:5

When I was thirteen, I returned from my daily subway commute to find family members gathered in front of my Brooklyn home. Uncle Guy put his arm around me and explained that my dad had been involved in an electrical accident. My mom was by his side when I arrived at the hospital. I'll never forget the fearful sight of seeing my dad's hands and face bandaged because they were burned.

The electrical flash burned his eyes, and he could no longer see. When the doctors held a bright light to his face, he could feel the heat on his neck, but when they asked if he could see anything, he said he was unable to. Luckily, his beard protected his lower face from being burned. The eye specialist informed us that it was possible he could recover sight in one eye, but it would involve healing and time.

That night, after returning to a home without Dad, my mom gathered my brothers and me into her room and asked us to kneel and pray to God for healing. We joined my mom in prayer with our all hearts. We recited the Lord's Prayer and asked God to heal my dad's sight.

The next day at the hospital my mother was met by an excited eye specialist. He held her hand and asked if she believed in miracles because my dad's sight had been completely restored overnight. An assurance that God was with us and heard our prayers for my dad's miraculous recovery set the groundwork for what would occur years later—after which my life would never be the same.

Those years later, I was at Northwestern Prep School. In addition to preparing students academically for the Air Force Academy, the school also helped us condition our bodies. Basic Cadet training included intense physical workouts. One day while jogging, I noticed my crucifix missing from my gold chain. The cross was a gift from my aunt and held sentimental value.

I was frantically retracing my steps, looking for the cross alongside a road, when a young man approached me. He asked if I needed help. After he helped me search for some time, we arrived at the end of the road and decided to rest under the shade of a massive tree. The young man began explaining the various wonders around me that I was too busy to notice. He encouraged me to observe my surroundings and really see the beauty of this world and to look at the big picture.

"Examine the texture of this grass," he challenged me, and he said, "Do you think that this butterfly's colors were made through evolution or intelligent design?"

He asked if I believed in God and if I knew of His Son, Jesus Christ. He passionately shared gospel stories about Jesus healing people and raising the dead back to life. He held a peace that I craved. I politely listened and left considering all that he talked about. My soul was moved by this young man's message, servant's attitude, and gentle spirit. Afterward, while alone, I asked God into my life and accepted the simple message that Jesus is the Son of God, and that He died for my sins.

I don't know if the young man helping me look for my cross was sent to help me find the Man who had been placed on the cross, but I do know that because he shared the gospel, I was moved to believe. Through the years, I've grown in my faith, and it begins with starting the day strong in prayer and reading the Scriptures. Life happens, and unforeseen events rock our world. Having a relationship with God empowers us when life seems out of control.

While in the military, it's likely that your courage will be tested while serving in combat zones. What you may see and experience there will require all you've got. During my first combat mission as a new officer after graduating from the Air Force Academy, I experienced a near-death encounter when my B-52 aircraft almost hit the ground while avoiding enemy fire. Faith in God and the assurance that my salvation was secure enabled me to find courage to keep going forward when everything inside of me wanted to hide. That faith stems from having a personal relationship with God through

Jesus and trusting in God's Word. By starting strong, I am equipped to handle with a sense of peace life's crises as they occur. I can't imagine not having a relationship with God under life's stressful conditions, let alone during combat.

As my favorite motivational speaker Clebe McClary says, "There are two types of fools in this world, fools for Jesus and fools for everyone else." You can label me as a fool for Jesus. Clebe was one of those men God placed in my life. As a Vietnam veteran who was severely wounded, he found amazing strength through the hope that comes through knowing Jesus, and he encourages all those around him. The question that Clebe and I ask is this: "Whose fool are you?"

If you don't know the Lord yet or don't understand that "peace that transcends all understanding" (Philippians 4:7), then please consider a relationship with Jesus. Believe in the Lord Jesus Christ, and you will be saved (Acts 16:31).

My dad losing his sight after an accident taught me the hope and power that comes through heartfelt prayer. As a young man in Santa Barbara, California, I lost my crucifix, but found faith because a stranger along the road was bold enough not to care what others thought. He shared the message of salvation to a young man who was lost. When survival seemed bleak during my first combat mission, knowing that God would never abandon me gave me the strength to overcome all obstacles, even death.

The greatest lesson I have ever learned is that the key to life is sacrifice. As a service man or woman, you know what sacrificing for your country means. Some of our fellow warriors have sacrificed their very lives for freedom. Your sacrifice and the sacrifice of those who have gone before you have ensured and continue to preserve America's freedom. Jesus' ultimate sacrifice of choosing to die for our sins assures *eternal freedom* to those who believe in Him. So, if you're lost, if you're blind, if you're longing for answers when life's burdens weigh you down, pray. God is waiting for you to find the cross along your path, and He will be the light, which removes blindness so you will see eternal hope.

Lord God, I need You. You alone know my heart. I am lost without You. Help me to find the hope that comes from believing in You. Reveal yourself in my life, and light my every day.

ARE YOU STARTING STRONG DAILY by reading the Scriptures? How much time do you spend conversing with God in prayer? Have you accepted the simple message that God sent His Son to die for the salvation of all who believe?

TEN

PMS—The Kind You Want

Maintaining Balance at Home

Finally, brothers and sisters, whatever is true, whatever is noble, whatever is right, whatever is pure, whatever is lovely, whatever is admirable—if anything is excellent or praiseworthy—think about such things.

Philippians 4:8

Can you guess this wonderful event? It grabs your attention with a rainbow of symptoms: your belt doesn't buckle; an internal hammer pounds within the depths of your gut and often, cranium; family members flee to anywhere that is not within fifty feet of your voice; you crave any food over a thousand calories, and you will take anyone hostage who tries to block you from getting it; you painfully flinch as your bra hooks are clasped together; your moods are as steady as walking a greased tightrope blindfolded. Every female undoubtedly recognizes the topic that I describe. It's PMS, and everyone, including males, dreads its onset.

However, there is another kind of PMS that will change your life for the better; it catalyzes what many only dream of experiencing—peace. This PMS is not gender specific. When utilized, restful sleep occurs, the jean size you've always hoped for finally fits, everyone gravitates to the human magnet you've become, and daily stress and worry are reduced, even eliminated. The PMS I speak of is the triangle of *physical, mental,* and *spiritual balance,* and it *is* achievable. Once obtained, you will say *adios* to negative thoughts and greet each day with renewed hope and joy.

Just as airline passengers are instructed by the flight attendant to apply oxygen to themselves first before administering it to children, you *must* learn to attend to your own physical, mental, and spiritual needs before you can effectively care for family members and fellow service personnel, execute successful missions, and achieve life goals. So get ready to have PMS! You will never walk past the personal hygiene section at the commissary or grocery store with the same mind-set again.

Physical. I love the Steven Covey-inspired story about two woodsmen competing for the same lumberjack position. To test their skills, their employer asked both lumberjacks (we'll call them Brody and Denver) to chop wood. They began working at dawn. Brody chopped straight through till noon without even a five-minute break. After he downed his lunch of a sandwich and chips within ten minutes, he rushed back to splitting logs. Sweat drenched his clothes. His muscles ached, but by the time the sun set, Brody stood back and admired his large pile of cut wood. Surely, he thought, *I will win the position.*

Denver began at sunrise, as well; however, he interrupted every hour like the headline news for a ten-minute rest. At lunch, he relaxed for a half hour and then returned to work, continuing to rest hourly. At sunset, Denver piled his wood next to Brody's stack. Denver's stack towered over Brody's. Perplexed, Brody asked, "How is it that I took only one break the entire day, and you rested every hour, and your stack exceeds mine?" Denver replied, "Easy. Each time I took a break, I sharpened my axe."

Do you take time to sharpen your axe? Besides taking care of family responsibilities, warriors also focus on their mission. Home-front spouses are notorious for placing themselves last on the "To Do" list; that is, if they even make the list! Add deployments to the mix, and self-care is only a magazine headline seen in the grocery store checkout aisle. So, it's time to ask yourself: *Do I find time to exercise? Do I sleep peacefully and for the required hours to feel rested? Do I binge when I'm nervous or skip meals when busy?* After self-evaluation, you may need some axe sharpening.

How many times have we heard this question: Have you made your health a priority? Enroll in an exercise fitness program on post/base or at a local gym. Patriotic business owners love to support our military. Ask them to work a deal for military members. Alternately, video workouts accommodate busy schedules, sidestepping gym or childcare requirements. Prioritizing health as No. 1 on your "To Do" list benefits not only you but also your coworkers, friends, and your entire family.

Trouble sleeping? Prescribed sleep medication became my crutch for three years due to stress-induced insomnia. While sharpening my axe with exercise, I researched how to balance hormones through diet, which affected sleep. Phasing out caffeine and minimizing preservatives (this means limiting fast food—ouch!) helped me to sleep through the night. It's a fact that when your body is tired, your metabolism doesn't burn calories effectively. Rest affects weight as well as mood and productivity.

"As iron sharpens iron, so one person sharpens another" (Proverbs 27:17). So, ask a friend to be your accountability partner to sharpen your physical goals. Make sure that in addition to being a faithful cheerleader, this friend will drag you to the treadmill when you'd rather slump in front of the latest DVD release while chomping down a double-cheese pizza. Sign an accountability contract together. Include your goals. Take before and after pictures (hide them from the prankster child who would jokingly post them on Facebook) and be inspired as you progress. Designate a reward when you reach your goal. When I challenged myself to lose twenty pounds, I rewarded myself with a few new outfits when I reached my goal. Your reward doesn't have to be clothes. Perhaps a massage or weekend getaway is more your thing. Have fun achieving the first part of PMS, and remember: If you don't "axe," you won't receive!

Mental. Surround yourself with positiveness, especially during deployments. Limit the media's bombardment of bad news, and hem yourself in with positive affirmations and encouraging people. The wise man of Scripture, Solomon, wrote, "For as he thinks in his heart, so is he" (Proverbs 23:7, New King James Version). When we fill our minds with good messages, wholesome television shows, and inspirational books—and couple them with encouraging friendships—we become more positive ourselves. Memorize Scripture and motivational quotes. Tape them to your mirrors and in your car. Staying connected with uplifting friends wards off isolation, which leads to loneliness and depression. Mark Twain's quote eloquently expresses this concept: "Keep away from people who try to belittle your ambitions. Small people always do that, but the really great make you feel that you too can become great." This doesn't mean you can't include the negative Nellies in your social gatherings, but just make sure your certitude influences them and not vice versa. If not, pray about exploring new friendships.

Spiritual. Spiritual balance completes our desired PMS triangle. Increasingly, scientific studies reveal that prayer and meditation positively affect one's physical and emotional well being. The strongest evidence, of course, is personal experience. Faith changed my life after Tony shared with us the news every military family dreads: "I'm leaving in two days. I can't tell you where and for how long. It may be six months, maybe longer. I'll let you know when I can." Joining a Bible study with other military members strengthened my faith during that first deployment and every military separation that followed. Reading inspirational daily devotions required only minutes each day yet kept me spiritually exercised. Not only did these activities strengthen me during deployments, but they also helped me overcome everyday stress, future marital trials, and health challenges. Reading and studying Scripture each day assures me that I am never alone. I walk through each new day knowing that God loves me and will care for my every need.

Dear Lord, some days I feel so unbalanced with life's pressures that I'm amazed I can walk! Help me to prioritize my physical, mental, and spiritual needs so I can shine Your love through me as a spouse, parent, leader, coworker, son/daughter, and a friend.

WHAT ARE YOU DOING to attain PMS balance? Discuss with your spouse/parent/friend the areas where you may be teetering and could use support to balance. What obstacles are preventing you from experiencing joy? Write down three specific goals to help achieve PMS. Then begin implementing them today.

Resources

See appendix C for daily devotional recommendations and Bible study helps.

ELEVEN

Prep the Battle Space of the Mind

Readying for Deployments

Do not conform to the pattern of this world, but be transformed by the renewing of your mind. Then you will be able to test and approve what God's will is—his good, pleasing and perfect will.

Romans 12:2

While stationed in Europe, my family and I traveled to France and viewed the sights of the historic World War II Battle of Normandy. We visited the beaches where Allied Forces bravely launched the beginning of the end of the Nazi regime by employing thousands of men against heavily fortified German defenses. We met with heroes who were on the battlefield during D-Day on June 6, 1944, and we stood on the hallowed grounds where thousands of our fellow Americans warriors are laid to rest. It's an amazing sight, and you can't help but be moved by their sacrifices.

While standing on the top of the cliffs, inside huge craters formed from shells of the allied battleships, I kneeled down and tried imagining what those brave men were thinking as they prepared for the greatest invasion of all time. Ships were crammed with people sick from the turbulent seas, airborne soldiers were jumping into the night skies against incoming antiaircraft artillery, and entire units of brave men were facing head-on the challenges of the unknown with tenacity and fierce determination. Each warrior had to dig deep and prepare his mental state for the upcoming conflict. As an airman who experienced similar fears of the unknown prior to launching combat strikes against a formidable enemy during Desert Storm, I can somewhat relate with those pressures. During my first combat mission while only a lieutenant, that fear of the unknown wreaked havoc on my mind. Did I have the courage to fight? Would I die tomorrow?

If you wear a military uniform, it's likely that you already have or likely will experience the immense mental pressure of entering the combat zone and facing this fear of the unknown. You'll need to prep the battle space of your mind to enable yourself to be victorious in battle and achieve mission success. Being afraid of an unseen enemy can be debilitating. As you get ready for deployments and new adventures, your preparedness will help you overcome fear. Developing a positive mental state will help you find courage to fight. The mental toughness gained from overcoming your fears will empower you to achieve greater things in life, when all hope seems lost to everyone else. Not you. You will be strong. You will view life with a new perspective. Almost every other pressure you will face pales in comparison to fighting in combat.

Many of the challenges I encountered prior to going to war dealt with battles within my own mind. Prior to finding the courage to fight, I wrestled with many "what if" scenarios. I found it necessary to clear these obstacles that clouded my judgment. I'd like to share those techniques, which worked for me, and can for you, as well.

Although this may seem contrary to positive thinking, plan for the worst and hope for the best. During deployments, I've been with warriors who were hurrying to make last-minute plans to complete a will or power of attorney. That's not the best time to do so. Give prior thought to these things, and ensure that your family is protected with adequate life insurance.

I wrote letters to loved ones and keep them in a private place. During a post-traumatic stress disorder conference in Houston, Texas, I met the parents of a fallen hero. They carried with them the last letter received from their son while he was serving in the Middle East. The patriot's letter was filled with how much he loved them, and he thanked his father for being such a wonderful dad. His parents were so proud of their son's service, and they thanked God for his life. His letter brought some healing to this wonderful couple who were inspired by their son's service. They are now helping other grieving parents of lost warriors.

Prior to deploying, try resolving any disputes. Do you have pent-up feelings that are weakening your marriage? Battleproof your marriage by taking the "Communication Tune-Up for Couples" in appendix A. If you're not at peace with your family or friends, don't think that distance will bring healing. It won't. I've met servicemen who have returned to an empty home after deploying because they didn't address the issues gnawing on their relationships beforehand. Be sure to control your emotions and avoid being arrogant or dominating. Listen to your spouse's point of view, and do your best to find common ground. Talk about ways you can communicate once deployed. And be patient, for your family is likely very emotional and worried for your upcoming deployment.

Spend quality time with your children before leaving, and plan on taking them somewhere special upon returning. Fortunately, many American institutions value our military by giving free tickets to theme parks such as Busch Gardens and Sea World. Children are very resilient, but they'll miss you something fierce, as will you them. Leave them something special, such a unit insignia or a name tape. Remind them that you serve with the best military in the world, and that you're ready to do your part to help defend America. They will sense your confidence, so make sure they know you are ready.

Has someone betrayed you and is in need of forgiveness? Find it in your heart to forgive that person. Conversely, seek forgiveness from those you've wronged. Combat quickly places relationships in the proper perspective. Major General Bob Dees's book *Resilient Warriors* is loaded with techniques for bouncing back when things don't go as planned and for dealing with the pressures of war. Major General Dees is a remarkable warrior-leader who has dedicated his life to serving military families. In his books on resiliency, he explains the importance of being more like a tennis ball than an egg. He describes that you have to work on that type of resiliency before, during, and after deployments to make you an effective warrior.

During combat, you're likely to witness disturbing events or be under intense pressures. The best preventive medicine to avoid post-traumatic stress disorder (PTSD) is educating yourself and your family before, during, and after deployment. Also, find Christian warriors who will pray alongside you and who will keep your faith sharpened. If you are familiar with PTSD symptoms, then you'll be equipped to help yourself and your team to take quick action against this debilitating challenge. (See "Combat-Related Stress Helps" in appendix B.) Trained professionals, chaplains, and commanders are available to lend a helping hand, so don't go at it alone. Be serious when you prep the battle space of your mind.

Last and most important, find peace in your own mind. One of the best resources I've found to help me achieve this goal was compiled by Dr. Kerry Spackman, a sports psychologist. His research and practical advice charts a road map for mental success. His techniques on understanding how the mind functions and his methods for rewiring it work for me. Dr. Spackman explains that our brain has a logical side and an emotional side, and the emotional side is stronger. If you control your emotional side to act more logically, then you will be more likely to succeed. To help me prep my mental battle space, I seek balance physically, mentally, and spiritually. I encourage you to prep your mind before engaging in actual warfare and deal with any obstacle that's preventing you from experiencing peace. The battle space in your mind is where wars are won. By developing mental toughness, you can focus energy on the tasks at hand.

If you're able to overcome mistakes and believe that you can succeed, then you likely will. By prepping your mind, you are on a path that leads to victory. And winning is a whole lot better than losing. The men and women who served before us and fought battles have had to face their fears.

The warriors during D-Day had no guarantees what the next day held. If you wear a military uniform, then the reality is that you'll likely face this fear of the unknown. Be prepared. Know your job. Value who you are. Plan for the worst-case scenario and make peace with those you love. God gave you the heart of a warrior for a purpose. He instilled certain talents, and now it's up to you to give your all when your best is required.

If you don't have a personal relationship with God, then there's no better time than now to seek peace with the Lord. Chaplains are a tremendous asset for our military and are there specifically for you. They're trained and equipped for this purpose, so don't think you're wasting their time. This is their profession, and they find it personally rewarding helping warriors find peace with God. Having that blessed assurance that your eternal life is secure will give you courage to fight.

Remember that when Jesus faced the Devil He recited Scripture to combat the Enemy's attacks. Memorizing Scripture was good enough for Jesus; then it's likely good enough for us all. One of my favorite Bible verses that helped me during my first combat deployment was "The Lord is my strength and my defense; he has become my salvation"(Psalm 118:14). With the hope that comes through God, you will be comforted in knowing that you are not alone.

Combat demands a level of attention that you've never faced before. You'll see things that will stay with you forever. How you react under extreme pressure is paramount to success and will define you in the future. You are one of America's guardians of freedom. You stand behind many great warriors who have faced giants and great odds, and won. No matter if your battle takes place in combat, on the home front, or in the workplace, when you prepare your mental state for victory before the time comes, you will be victorious.

Give me courage, God, to face the fear of the unknown. Be with me, Lord, as I prepare for whatever combat lies ahead.

ARE YOU READY FOR COMBAT? What have you done to prepare the battle space of your mind? Is there anyone you need to ask forgiveness from or need to forgive yourself?

Resources

Resilient Warriors by Major General Bob Dees (US Army, Ret.) provides relevant, enduring principles of resilience for warriors in every foxhole of life, and urgently needed information and inspiration to help us recover from the wounds of the past, weather the storms of the present, and build resilience for the future challenges.

Psalm 118:5–17

When hard pressed, I cried to the Lord; he brought me into a spacious place.
The LORD is with me; I will not be afraid. What can mere mortals do to me?

The LORD is with me; he is my helper. I look in triumph on my enemies.

It is better to take refuge in the LORD than to trust in humans.

It is better to take refuge in the LORD than to trust in princes.

All the nations surrounded me, but in the name of the LORD I cut them down.

They surrounded me on every side, but in the name of the LORD I cut them down.

They swarmed around me like bees, but they were consumed as quickly as burning thorns; in the name of the LORD I cut them down.

I was pushed back and about to fall, but the LORD helped me.

The LORD is my strength and my defense; he has become my salvation.

Shouts of joy and victory resound in the tents of the righteous: "The LORD's right hand has done mighty things!

The LORD's right hand is lifted high; the LORD's right hand has done mighty things!"

I will not die but live, and will proclaim what the LORD has done.

PART 3

Combat-Related Stress Care

TWELVE

Here I Stand in the Middle of Serenity

Controlling Anger

No one pours new wine into old wineskins. Otherwise, the
new wine will burst the skins; the wine will run out and
the wineskins will be ruined.

Luke 5:37

"Rerouting" was all I heard from our GPS as we weaved through Los Angeles traffic in a crammed rental car while on our first family vacation in years. As a pilot, knowing where I'm going is a prerequisite, so a detour commanded by a mechanical device upset me. "Turn right next off ramp" was all I heard over the background music and laughter from the kids in the backseat. "Not this off ramp, the next one," chimed in Penny. After a U-turn, we were back on track and the ocean was in view.

Our route led us to a neighborhood that shouted "Look out!" Most of the businesses had long, prison-like bars on the windows.

To distract my family from my uneasiness and after locking the car doors, I reminded everyone not to forget the hats in the trunk.

The previous day had been a momentous one as our son Nico graduated from Chapman University. The complementary hats were a reminder of his academic accomplishment. I was proud of him and looked forward to proudly wearing the Chapman hat. When we finally entered the cruise ship embankment area, the GPS triumphantly announced, "You have arrived at your destination." However, we were at the wrong ship. The Carnival Cruise ship was in plain sight, but a barrier separated us from it. After yet a few more U-turns, we finally made it to the correct gate.

When we arrived, an enthusiastic team of Carnival employees swarmed our car and quickly unloaded the luggage. I could tell from the look on Penny's face that she was not happy. She likely was concerned that the old Tony, the guy who would get angry when things didn't go as planned, would resurface. Years earlier, I would have added many Brooklyn expletives to the way I was feeling. I had changed since my younger years, but not completely, mind you. Penny could tell that something was brewing inside me. Did I mention that we forgot the hats in the trunk?

After waiting in a long line alongside a woman who was cursing up a storm about her no-good husband who had abandoned her for one of her girlfriends, my anxiety got worse. Antonio, possessing protective instincts, attempted to shield his little sister from the irate woman. Normally, I would have had compassion and listened to her ordeal, but based on her spiteful talk, I just wanted to get on the boat, look at the ocean as the boat was going to wherever, and relax.

After posing for the mandatory mug shots that would cost hundreds of dollars upon debarkation, we finally made it onto the boat and into cabin R86. We were shocked to find that it was possible for a family of five to fit in a room the size of a prison cell. After discovering that two bunk beds came out of the wall and a small bed was hidden in the closet, we realized that we had about a two-by-four-foot living area. More elaborate rooms were available, but I was on a military salary and had just paid for a graduation dinner that cost more than our monthly mortgage.

Penny suggested we tour the boat, and we agreed to go our separate ways and reconnect with the kids at 8:15 at our assigned dining room table. I looked forward to enjoying dinner with a nice ocean view, where we could have family time. When we arrived at table 225, however, it wasn't the private booth with a scenic view that I envisioned. Instead, it was a large round table, seating twelve, in the middle of the dining room. Oh well, I figured; just go with it. But just then a tidal wave of a personality hit our table like a tsunami. Jack was holding an oversized beer in one hand and an attractive, clearly younger, low-cut-dress-wearing woman on the other. He was, shall I say, a bit loud. My daughter Gabriella raised her eyebrows.

During our ensuing conversation with Jack, he mentioned that he was a retired airborne ranger trained by marines back in 'Nam. I doubted his claims and challenged his remarks.

When "Stan the Man," our maître d', who claimed to be from Louisiana while touting an English accent and clearly being of Pakistani descent, stopped by, he asked, "Why all the long faces?" I knew that our small group was not having a good time. Penny looked at me as my dad would when angry. Her scrunched lips resembled a pucker fish. Obviously, the mood shifted badly.

Two-by-two everyone left, and I found myself alone at this huge round table surrounded by free alcoholic beverages. It would have been way too easy for me to have a drink or two in order to ease the tension and hang loose with Jack and his cute girlfriend. But I knew that drinking brought out the tiger in me, so I avoided the temptation and made my way to the back of the boat.

With an ice water hosting a lone lime in hand, I found myself alone, watching the waves churned by the ship's powerful engines. Through the scattering clouds, I saw glimmers of the moon. The fragrance from the ocean always sedates my soul, and I took a deep breath of the ocean air. Then it happened. I looked down almost out of a sense of desperation while wondering why I was so uptight. After all, Jack was just having a good time, and my family forgetting hats in the trunk was no big deal in the grand scheme of things. What was the problem?

While bowing my head down, I prayed silently to God to help me relax. After opening my eyes, I realized that I was standing in the center of a circle with the word *Serenity* surrounding the circumference. So there I was, standing in the middle of *serenity* on a boat going to wherever. While cracking a smile, I closed my eyes and gave thanks to God for listening to my prayers and bringing me to this special spot. I had finally made it. I decided right there and then that my vacation would now begin. The old Tony would not arise, and the new one could take comfort in knowing that while not perfect,

I was at peace with myself for striving to do the right thing. Anger would not ruin my life or those around me, nor would I give in to the temptation of drinking alcohol in order to have a good time.

Since that fateful day, one of the best techniques I have used to combat anger is to view a picture of a chained German Shepherd dog, gnarling while displaying his fangs. The image reminds me of the "old Tony," the angry dog. No one, and I mean no one, wants to go near a barking, wild dog. If I grow angry, I envision myself as that mean dog, and the thought causes me to cringe. It triggers an emotional response that reminds me that my angry outbursts have destructive effects on others. I no longer want to be like an angry dog. I prefer standing in the middle of serenity, and the new picture in my mind is one of peace. New wine going into new wineskins, not new wine going into old wineskin (Mark 2:22). If the old Tony were to come back, the result would be like a bursting wineskin that would cause a mess. No more messes, please.

When someone is angry and if that person is unaware of his or her behavior, he or she may say and do things that a rational person would never dream of. A technique that works for me is to walk away when upset. If my body alerts me that I'm getting angry, such as when my heart races or my muscles become tense, then I remove myself from the situation. I've asked Penny to signal me when she notices any signs of anger. Her signal is a funny one, and it's hard being angry when smiling. After receiving and acknowledging her warning, I remove myself from the area and cool off. We all have issues, and life is too short to cause pain. In my case, I decided to change my behavior.

I've found that when people get angry, their blood pressure rises and adrenaline kicks in. Anger and stress cause the body to tighten and muscles to tense up. Anger can cause sleep disorders and numerous medical issues, such as gastrointestinal problems and depression, to name just a few. How a person deals with anger affects physical health and mental well-being.

If you are struggling with anger problems, seek help from a counselor or chaplain. They're professionally trained to help people with anger management. Most people know if they have anger issues; some are just too proud to admit it. If your family says you do, then you likely do.

The best thing that works for me is to remove myself from the situation. Just walk away. Avoid the use of excessive caffeine, for that can provoke anxiety and lead to anger. Try to find out what triggers your anger, and develop means to recognize those triggers. Exercising regularly relieves stress, so develop daily workout routines.

Sometimes, anger is justifiable. Even Jesus got angry. Ever read the Bible story about Jesus overturning tables and driving people out that were desecrating the house of God?

There will be U-turns in life, and lost hats, but to remain steadfast toward improving self in the face of challenges takes courage and fortitude.

I was committed to change and apologized to Jack for my remarks, and I thoroughly enjoyed the rest of my family vacation, and so did everyone else. We made some great new acquaintances at the dinner table while enjoying the exquisite foods. Jack turned out to be a great guy, and "Stan the Man" was a riot. I went dancing, rode horses with the family on beautiful beaches, and had a blast by the pool. And I never resorted to any alcohol to have a "good time." My vacation started that moment in time on the back of the boat to wherever, and so did my new life direction as I pondered, "Here I stand in the middle of serenity."

Lord God, grant me peace. Help me to not give in to anger. Teach me Your ways and guide me to be a good person. Help me to be in control of my emotions.

HOW ABOUT YOU? Do you struggle with anger? Are you in a relationship with someone who is angry? Do you resort to alcohol or drugs to help you relax when things are too stressful? Have you committed to not going to the old self and choosing instead to do the right thing? What are some positive ways that you can defuse anger when you feel it approaching?

THIRTEEN

Flea from Worry and Fear

Exterminating Anxiety

Submit yourselves, then, to God. Resist the devil, and he will flee from you.

James 4:7

After venting daily to my sister, Pam, about our horrendous flea infestation that interfered with writing as this book's deadline approached with the speed of an oncoming train, she encouraged me, "A story exists in there somewhere. You have to write about it!" Pam was right, "All things work together for good to those who love God, to those who are called according to His purpose" (Romans 8:28, New King James Version). But next time, Lord, please use something nicer than fleas to convey your point.

Eight acres of beautiful, wooded land grace the view from our living room windows. We are also blessed to own two wonderful long-haired dogs: Stella, our Golden Retriever; and Yukon Cornelius, a Bernese Mountain Dog appropriately named after the scatter-brained gold prospector from *Rudolph, the Red-Nosed Reindeer.* The country and big dogs usually fit together like ducks and water; however, when a record-breaking warm winter mixes with a scorching drought the following summer, a skyrocketing bug population results. The combination, we soon discovered, was mentally and physically exhausting.

The veterinarian first attributed Yukon's itching to food allergies. We changed dog foods and then left the next day for a ten-day vacation. When we returned and my daughter said, "Eww, Mom, what are those black things crawling on the dogs?" I knew we were in trouble. By then, it was too late. Like marathon runners sprinting forth at the starting gun's blast, these little critters dashed in droves from our thick shag carpet onto our ankles, clothing, and furniture. I nearly dialed 911 until my son assured me that policemen don't carry flea pesticide. The United States was battling the second worst drought in history over the lower 48 states (according to CNN) as Missouri headed into its third week of temperatures exceeding 100 degrees. The dogs had to remain inside for their safety.

I soon forged great friendships with Jill, the pest control company's business manager, and three veterinarians as we strategized daily how to destroy the battalion of fleas.

My flea knowledge soon exceeded any encyclopedia's information as I spent days searching the Internet, soaking in any useful data to get rid of the nasty creatures. For instance, I learned that several pounds of Borax detergent sifted and then raked into carpets and left for 48 hours doesn't kill as advertised. Instead, the granules create a non-skid flea dance floor. Trust me, I watched the little varmints do the two-step!

I also discovered that I morbidly find pleasure in witnessing fleas discover their fate. I looked forward to watching them dive into one of my thirteen concocted death traps of soapy, water-filled pans illuminated by a desk lamp, which underhandedly lured them to "go toward the light." As the fleas dove into the dishes of death, my cheers could be heard from the baseball field down the street. (In case you wondered, it only takes five seconds for a flea to drown.)

Each flea produces two hundred eggs, and although vacuuming helps eliminate the population, the vibrations it creates stimulates eggs to hatch. The last fun fact is that fleas can carry nasty diseases that transmit to dogs and humans.

I discovered that certain medications can sterilize future flea offspring, but it takes months to depopulate the flea community. Plus, the stuff costs as much as a month's worth of groceries for a family of five.

My dreams were haunted by car-sized fleas clobbering my door and heckling my dishes of death. Nipping fleas disturbed my tranquil writing routine, caused anxiety, and stole my peace. I became obsessed with the fleas and spent hours vacuuming daily.

Finally, I surrendered my flea infestation to prayer and called for reinforcements. Prayer warrior friends and family interceded. My mom's colorful prayer routine consists of swimming prayer laps. (God hears us wherever we are, and I envision Him smiling with my mom's every stroke.) My friend Marshele encouraged me with the humorous but true verse heading this chapter. Combating the flea attacks with prayer restored my peace, and I returned to writing. After four exterminations by two different pest control companies within one month, treating our dogs with pills, sprays, mists, shampoos, collars, oils, and flea-zapping electric combs, I learned that exterminating fleas requires patience, daily housekeeping, total determination, and professional guidance.

Looking back, I see that God truly does use all situations for His purpose. Our exterminator was a Vietnam veteran suffering from PTSD. Because of the severity of the infestation, more pest-control visits were required than normal. He and I talked for hours and I was able to share healing resources and the hope that comes through Christ.

All of the queried veterinarians told me the fleas would be eliminated, but because of where we lived, a wooded location, we should expect future outbreaks. They assured me that had I not treated our dog and home, the fleas would have overtaken us. Eliminating fear, worry, and anxiety from our lives is like exterminating unwanted fleas. When our children sign on the dotted line to join the military, our ears automatically become magnetized to negative military news and headlines like a flea attracted to light. As our spouses and military family members deploy, our hearts deploy alongside them with a platoon of debilitating emotions that steal our peace and prevent us from being productive. Visions of veterans returning with physical and invisible wounds haunt our dreams; we wonder if our loved one will remain safe. Just when we think we have captured the anxieties with our homemade concoctions of staying overly busy, self-medications, and addictive behaviors, such as overspending, unhealthy eating, etc., the drove of negative thoughts bites us. Like disease-carrying fleas, anxiety and fear can transmit anger, depression, stress-induced illnesses, and much more. Thankfully, like my peace-stealing pests, worry and fear can be exterminated with daily, diligent prayer, patience with God's timing, and confidence that a "professional" is ultimately in control. God is the true Orkin anxiety killer, and if we open our hearts, we will see God's blessings through the trials.

Whenever Tony deployed and negativity gnawed at my thoughts, I exterminated them with 2 Corinthians 10:5 and learned that I could make my thoughts align themselves with God's commands not to worry. That verse assures me: "We demolish arguments and every pretension that sets itself up against the knowledge of God, and we take captive every thought to make it obedient to Christ."

Peace drowns worry and fear. The Devil enjoys multiplying your worries like infesting fleas to prevent you from living abundantly and being productive. I know now through our flea experience and other recent events that completing this book was under attack by Enemy forces, so Tony and I claimed authority through Scripture, which God empowers us with to eliminate the adversary: "I have given you authority to trample on snakes and scorpions and to overcome all the power of the enemy; nothing will harm you" (Luke 10:19). I mentally added fleas to the verse.

Notice that Luke says we can overcome "all" the power of the Enemy. Not just bits and fragments, but *everything* that is stealing our peace. God gives us dominion through His sovereignty to overcome any and all attacks.

Eliminate negative thoughts through daily housekeeping. Like the dormant flea eggs that hatch with vibration, anxiety and fear breed when agitated with stressors, such as war, illness, violence, and injustice, which infest our peace. Just as the wooded property will cause us to constantly battle native pests, we will always be fighting these anxiety-producing adversaries because of where we live—a sinful world. But we can rest knowing that the One true professional, God, assures victory.

"I have told you these things, so that in me you may have peace. In this world you will have trouble. But take heart! I have overcome the world" (John 16:33).

Dear Lord, thank You for being in control of all situations in my life when I feel helpless. Please strengthen me when worry and fear infest my peace. Help me to experience the peace that comes from trusting You.

TRY THIS NEGATIVE THOUGHT PESTICIDE: For every one fearful thought, list ten reasons you are thankful. Post them on a mirror or other regularly viewed area to remind you daily that God is in control and that your prayers exterminate all enemies so peace can prevail.

FOURTEEN

Seek Common Ground

Embracing Diversity

After this I looked, and behold, a great multitude that no one could number, from every nation, from all tribes and peoples and languages, standing before the throne and before the Lamb, clothed in white robes, with palm branches in their hands, and crying out with a loud voice, "Salvation belongs to our God who sits on the throne, and to the Lamb!"

Revelation 7:9–10,
English Standard Version

"Welcome to the war zone, ladies!" joked my aircraft commander while we hunkered down to avoid incoming shots fired on our bus convoy in Saudi Arabia. But I'm getting ahead of myself.

Previously, after landing from a combat mission during Operation Desert Storm, a Middle Eastern customs control officer gave each crew member a handout listing restrictions while serving in

Saudi Arabia. Besides what you would expect of a Muslim nation's moral standards, which are mainly good values, I was surprised with an issued pamphlet. It clearly stated that the Muslim religion was the *only* true religion. The pamphlet acknowledged Jesus as a prophet but not the Son of God. It quoted New Testament Scriptures conveniently backing their claims, while intentionally overlooking other truths written in the Bible. As American service members stationed in Saudi Arabia, we were forbidden from sharing our faith with their citizens, yet they could share their faith with us. I found it ironic that Americans were restricted from basic freedoms while protecting their homeland from a Muslim dictator threatening their borders during Desert Storm. *Welcome to Saudi Arabia,* I thought. *What am I doing here?* My "welcome to Saudi Arabia" experience escalated during a bus ride from the flight line to our sleeping quarters.

My crew and I heard gunshots as the bus abruptly stopped. A machine-gun-toting US Marine boarded the bus and evacuated us. We all dove belly down once outside the bus. While we were lying on our stomachs, my aircraft commander Mike looked up and said, "Welcome to the war zone, ladies!" We all started cracking up nervously. There we were, thousands of miles from home—one minute eating pizza with our families in New York and now dodging bullets in the war zone. It was a surreal moment that I'll never forget. Laughing while terrified. Crazy.

A few days later, the jovial Saudi guard escorting us held up a local newspaper as if it were an Olympic gold medal. The two men who wounded a few American troops on the bus were allegedly punished by having an arm and opposite leg amputated. The mastermind behind the attack was beheaded in a public square. The guard proudly chanted, "See, Saudi justice!" I thought to myself, *These guys sure don't think like we do.* I was impressed that they caught the gunmen but amazed that they went through a trial and judgment so quickly. Could you imagine that happening in the USA? Being stationed overseas helps you learn about other customs while making you appreciate home.

Many of our world's problems stem from intolerance influenced by extremists. A twisted ideology can adversely shape a nation to do unthinkable atrocities. You only need look at Germany in the early 1940s to see what extremism can do. When you mix extremists with a military force, it can lead to disaster. Under Adolf Hitler's influence, the predominantly Christian nation of Germany, comprised of hard-working people, brutally oppressed many cultures, which led to the near extinction of the Jewish race. Extremism is deadly. Over the course of human history, religious extremists have taken over institutions, organizations, and nations causing havoc. These rogue agents use distorted hate ideology to manipulate and scare people into believing what they believe, or else.

During my stay in the Middle East, it was clear that the majority of Muslims are great people. It's the extremists that adversely infect individuals with hate ideology. The terrorist organization with such twisted beliefs of using airlines packed with innocent civilians as weapons, clearly demonstrates hatred in action. The terrorists who attacked America on 9/11 are a vivid reminder of the adverse effects of rogue agents and why it's vital to be aware of extremists and not overlook their potentially harmful effects. Not all governments influenced by religion are bad; they're just different from our American way of life that embraces God and clearly demands a freedom of religion—as written in the First Amendment to the US Constitution. While deployed as US servicemen, we should respect the culture of other nations and dignity of all peoples. We should act and speak respectfully.

Just as in World War II, our mission is to protect and defend our nation. This is why we serve. While serving we must refrain from the temptation of treating enemy forces or other cultures as second-rate citizens. My grandfather, who served in the Italian Armed Forces, expressed immense admiration for American GIs when taken prisoner of war during World War II in Africa. He was amazed that our soldiers treated him and his family with respect. After the war, my grandfather came to America with his family largely due to the way American soldiers treated him. As a result, my father remained in America and earned his citizenship.

When serving, we should be respectful of others' beliefs while staying true to our own convictions, for our actions can serve as a transformational tool. Our American values centered on freedom have and continue to make a positive difference. The images of seeing thousands of men and women in Iraq proudly display their purple index finger after voting for the first time in a free country after Operation Iraqi Freedom should serve as a motivator to all US service members that helped liberate Iraq. After World War II, our military helped transform a war-torn Europe and Japan into the democracies that are flourishing today. Rather than pillage and conquer nations, America has a tradition of leaving them better than we found them. It is the crazy zealots that attempt to force their beliefs on others that cause widespread pain and suffering.

While in uniform, I believe it's best to remain true to our oath of office. Live your faith through actions, love God, but avoid extremism. Many of our founding fathers were Christians who were proud of their moral beliefs. They ensured a separation of church and state, not church *from* state. They never thought to exclude God from their lives. They relied on the grace that God bestowed upon our nation. America prides itself on being a melting pot of various cultures and religions. America is awesome and we should continue, as patriots, to protect and love her. There is a minority that tries to take any reference of God out of our American way of life as if our founding fathers never meant to include God. These people go to great lengths, all in the name of protecting individual rights, to remove God. That's wrong. As service members, we have every right to stand up for our love of God and country.

On the opposite extreme, some professed Christians attend funeral services of fallen American warriors and chant hate words—all under the banner of Christ. How can followers of Jesus spew such insults against families in their darkest hour, when they should be receiving an outpouring of love? Could you ever imagine Jesus emulating that behavior? I tried understanding the beliefs of these "Christians." They believe God is punishing America for its sinful actions. To counter this belief, some veterans show up to the funerals to shield the grieving families from the insults. These patriots arrive on their motorcycles and bear large USA flags and sing patriotic songs as their weapons.

There are many worthwhile patriotic organizations that embrace American values while respecting cultural diversity. By meeting and joining forces with organizations such as Veterans of Foreign Wars,

American Legion and United Service Organization (USO), you can continue to be part of a team that helps build American values while supporting our military veterans.

As warriors, we have sworn an oath to protect and defend America and to obey the *lawful* orders of those appointed over us. It is not our responsibility to define politics or to align ourselves with extremist groups. We have to honor our oath of service. US service members have given their all to defend America, and some have paid the ultimate sacrifice with their very lives. We have a solemn obligation not to mix religion and politics with our profession of arms. While serving at various outposts of the world, we need to respect others' customs and be good ambassadors of America. How we behave and treat others will result in transforming positive results, as our rich history proves. After we retire or transition from the military, we should continue to stand for protecting America while choosing wisely who we align our values with, for she's worth protecting. Remember the sacrifices of those who have gone before us, and embrace cultural diversity while seeking common ground.

Heavenly Father, give me wisdom to live my faith while being respectful of others' beliefs. Help me not to judge others.

HOW DO YOU TREAT OTHERS who aren't cut from the same cloth as you? Do you harbor animosity toward a certain race, religion, or culture? How can you find common ground with others who are different from you?

FIFTEEN

Which Cross Will You Choose?

Struggling with Faith

"Are you not the Christ? Save yourself and us!"
Luke 23:39,
English Standard Version

"My dad was a chaplain and held such a deep faith before he went to Iraq. Now that he is home, he won't even go to church with us; he is bitter and angry at God." The college freshman's tears streamed down her face as she described her father's lost faith after he returned from the combat zone. "He's hardened his heart against God, and faith was always the one thing we could count on with dad. My mom is a mess. My dad moved out. What should my family and I do?"

Many service members are returning home with invisible scars. They may have witnessed combat and possibly the death of a trusted comrade. I've heard numerous firsthand accounts of warriors holding their friend's wounded body as they breathed their last breath. They question God, "If you are loving, why don't you stop this suffering?" Trained to obey leadership without questioning orders, warriors may wonder if risking physical and mental wounds, along with the strain deployments place on relationships, is worth the sacrifice. Christians along with nonbelievers are not immune to doubting the sovereignty of God.

Many of the biblical "greats" were plagued with the same doubts that our service members face today. Even Jesus pleaded to God before His imminent death, "Father, if you are willing, take this cup from me; yet not my will, but yours be done" (Luke 22:42).

The fact remains that when good men do nothing, evil prevails, and our country needs our servicemen and women to retain our freedoms. But where is God in this suffering? Why does He allow pain if He has the power to stop it?

So where is God when we suffer? Where is He when the doctor says, "Your seven-year-old daughter has cancer"? Where is He when your spouse says, "I don't love you anymore"? Where is He when the bank says, "I'm sorry. We have to foreclose on your home"? Where is He when a crazed gunman massacres innocent school children? Where is He when a warrior returns from the combat zone as a different person from the one who deployed? The answer is this: Look to the cross.

The thieves who were being crucified on crosses next to Jesus asked similar questions as they approached physical death. "One of the criminals hanging beside him scoffed, 'So you're the Messiah, are you? Prove it by saving yourself—and us, too, while you're at it!'" (Luke 23:39, New Living Translation). The man on the right, who was not only a thief but probably a murderer as well, realized his own brokenness and that he deserved punishment for his crime. The shackles of mental pain and spiritual doubt fell from his heart the moment he recognized his need for Jesus in his life. The advent of death still awaited him, but now, his inner soul soared free.

As my dear friend Lavonne and I drove to San Antonio's airport after squeezing in a beach trip to Corpus Christi's shoreline, a question chimed through the kneeboards-and-luggage-packed backseat. Tanner, my friend's awesome twelve-year-old son and self-made game show host, was announcing trivia answers from a website. "Did you know that Gestas and Dismas were the names of the two thieves that were crucified on the cross next to Jesus?" My ears perked since I had coincidentally begun writing this chapter (although I don't believe in coincidences). I replied, "No. I never thought about the thieves having names." Tanner's question resonated with me. Here were two men whose stories inspire readers worldwide about the importance of choosing eternal salvation, and their names were unimportant to me. But Jesus knew them. "Do not fear, for I have redeemed you; I have summoned you by name; you are mine" (Isaiah 43:1).

We are nameless to most of the world's population. But not to God. Our heavenly Father knows each one of us intimately. Every hair on our head is accounted for. He knows our struggles, our history, and the reasons we may doubt our faith. God's desire is for us to trust and believe in Him with our own free will—to surrender our pride, our uncertainties, our past hurts—and recognize our need for a Savior. Dismas, the thief to the right of Jesus, did. He could have died bitter over the world's sinful condition, blaming his upbringing, an absent parent, childhood trauma he experienced, or people who let him down in life. Yet he chose the living hope that believing in Jesus offered. In the book *When You Can't Find God* author Linda Evans Shepherd poses the question, "Are you seeking to change your circumstances more than you are seeking God? That's not a good idea, because one of the keys to surviving difficult times is to focus on Him, not our troubles."

Jesus yearns to remove that which blocks us from experiencing God's peace and love. If you have experienced or witnessed pain, sorrow, injustice, and are struggling to understand how God could allow such suffering, you are not alone, but dare to look further. Recognize your need for a Savior as Dismas did. We live in a world of sin and we mess up daily ourselves, but Jesus knows us by name. We will always have suffering in this world because of man's choice to sin from the beginning of time, as unfair as that may seem. But God does not "check out" of our lives when pain and heartache hit. He "checked in" to our world of suffering by becoming a man and dying on the cross. Whether we see the reasons for suffering within our lifetime or not, "God uses sinful circumstances for His redemptive good."[11]

Look to the cross. Gestas, to the left of Jesus, hurled insults at Christ. He taunted Jesus, demanding He show His power by freeing them if He were truly the Son of God. Gestas's cross led not only to a physical death but likely to an eternal one as well. Although Gestas's fate is unknown (we are not told that He trusted Jesus), Scripture clearly states that when Dismas stripped himself of his pride, recognized himself as a sinner, and revealed his belief in the Son of

---

11. Pastor Brian Classen, in a sermon given at First Baptist Church, Warrensburg, MO, June 17, 2012.

God, his future was immediately decided. Jesus said to him, "I tell you the truth, today you will be with me in paradise" (Luke 23:43 NIV, 1984). This thief's cross, although he would still die, led to hope and eternal life, and it renews our hope today.

Look to the cross. Recognizing Jesus Christ as Savior gave Dismas eternal salvation and peace. Sometimes, the revelation to believe in Christ surfaces through suffering due to the sin that lives alongside us, but salvation *is* a choice. You can choose to hang on to bitterness and pain that weighs your soul down for years and accept Jesus as Savior later in life, like Dismas, but why waste precious time? Give your heart and suffering over to the Lord today. Your belief will not spare you from the evil that reigns on this earth, but it will free you from the bondage that resides in your own heart, so you can experience the joy that only comes from knowing Christ. Which cross will you choose?

Dear heavenly Father, there are times when I struggle with my faith because of the sin I've seen in this world and the suffering that occurs. Reign in me, O Lord, when I can't understand. Forgive me of the sins I have committed. Release me from the bondage of doubt, and lead me to the spring of hope that comes from recognizing You as my Savior.

WHAT PAST PAINS ARE HOLDING YOU BACK from surrendering *all* to Jesus and experiencing joy and peace? Right now, lay that suffering at the foot of the cross. If you haven't already, ask Jesus into your life. If you doubt Christ's existence, you are not alone. Ask the Lord to reveal himself to you and increase your faith. Then get ready. He will.

Resource

When You Can't Find God: How to Ignite the Power of His Presence by Linda Shepherd. The storms of life visit us all, and at times we find ourselves ill prepared to weather them. Where is God when everything comes crashing down? Linda Evans Shepherd shows readers how to see God in any circumstance, even when it's hard, and offers strategies for surviving difficult times, giving your troubles to God, praying through the pain, and finding peace, hope, and joy once more.

SIXTEEN

Amazing Men

Finding Help and Healing After Combat

The groans of the dying rise from the city, and the souls of the wounded cry out for help. But God charges no one with wrongdoing.

Job 24:12

"Stop by the restaurant and meet some amazing men," my brother Giuliano exclaimed with his raw Brooklyn accent. You'd think that after ten years of living in the Midwest he'd lose his "Brooklynese." Anytime he gets excited about something, the accent goes into overdrive. He was fired up about something as I hurried into our quaint Italian Ristorante. It was past closing time, and Monetti's Pizzeria Ristorante would normally be in cleanup mode, but not that night. A team of touring "wounded warriors" was in town.

When I walked in, one of the veterans with burns on his face greeted me. He had a larger-than-life personality and a great smile. I looked him in the eyes and introduced myself as I shook his hand.

That same wounded warrior, Iraq war veteran J. R. Martinez, would later go on to win the coveted *Dancing with the Stars* competition. Millions viewed his dazzling smile and personality, and others could see what I saw that night: a great guy living large and infecting those around him with his optimistic personality.

Each wounded veteran shared inspiring war stories as my brother kept the exquisite Italian food coming. Giuliano was happy giving back to these special men who gave so much to our nation. My brother was treating them as family and just wanted to keep serving them to show respect in his own way. As one of the veterans with artificial limbs shared his combat experience, you could have heard a pin drop. I wondered how tough life must be for them and their families with their physical challenges.

These special warriors have one common attribute. They are determined not to let their disability get them down. Their attitude soared, and it was a source of their strength. By living large and helping others, they have victory against an enemy that tried destroying them, an enemy priding itself in hiding roadside bombs and in indiscriminately killing civilians and military alike. But the enemy failed to demolish these warriors' will to survive. If anything, it made these patriots stronger, and as a result of their strength of character, they encourage other warriors to be stronger still.

I knew this was a special night. We stayed open for hours and enjoyed the food and beverages while sharing war stories. J. R. Martinez explained that he respects that others have suffered a much worse fate than his. He was happy to be alive and helps others still suffering from the effects of war. His encouraging words fired me up. My brother was right; these guys are amazing men.

The outward scars of war can be seen by human eyes, but the inward scars, which are just as damaging, are harder to notice. Scarred faces and missing limbs are obvious, but the unseen wounds of war continuously cause havoc in the minds of warriors and can lead to severe depression. I interviewed an army sergeant who served three tours in Iraq. He shared stories of the horrors of war affecting wounded warriors as a result of post-traumatic stress disorder (PTSD). His unique story of triumph over tragedy motivates me, just as the wounded warriors at my restaurant did. As a result of our meetings with this warrior, who we'll call Sgt. Kenney to respect his privacy, and his lovely wife Ann, Penny and I gained a greater understanding of the challenges warriors and their families face. This is the story of an honorable soldier who returned from serving in the chaos of the Iraq War back to his hometown in Texas.

Sgt. Kenney loved serving in the army and being with the men in his unit. He was proud to be in the finest army in the world with the challenging mission of stabilizing war-torn Iraq. His direct orders resulted in the death of enemy forces. The incident that haunted Sgt. Kenney involved a young warrior under his care who committed suicide, likely due to relationship problems at home. Sgt. Kenney lost hope once this fine young man killed himself. He felt he could have somehow prevented it.

Upon returning home and trying to deal with normalcy while reliving traumatic events that occurred, life seemed beyond challenging. He found himself gripping the steering wheel of his car and hunkering down while speeding and weaving in and out of city traffic. In his mind, he was dodging improvised explosive devices (IEDs) in Baghdad. Ann couldn't understand him any longer. Why was he so different? What happened to the man she married? He used to be outgoing and happy; now he was despondent and spent most of his time isolated in his room. Their relationship was falling apart.

His idea of reconciliation was volunteering to return to the war zone. Sgt. Kenney wanted back, for it was in Iraq while serving in the army he loved that the world made sense. The army provided that structure. That discipline. Men had his back and he had theirs. The enemy was out there, and the chaos of war provided an adrenaline high. He needed that stress to get him to a place that made him feel accepted, normal.

While listening, I found myself going back to my own war experiences. As a former warrior who has faced near-death situations, I could relate. The constant vigilance means that your senses are at peak levels. You seem in tune with yourself and the men around you. The team gels and the mission focuses you toward doing something bigger than yourself. You want to be in the game and not be a spectator. In the States, people complain about trivial matters.

Sgt. Kenney wanted back to that place where he fit in. He wanted back now. But his wife and family needed him. While at home, they wanted him to be home, and not in Iraq or wherever he was in his own mind. It got so bad that Sgt. Kenney decided to take his own life, until Ann intervened.

What happened next is a miracle. Sgt. Kenney became involved with the PTSD Foundation of America, which specializes in providing hope and healing for the unseen wounds of war. This amazing organization helps bring healing to our veterans while raising awareness of the plight of many warriors. It provides a way for a warrior to network with government and nonprofit agencies. This organization and counselors helped Sgt. Kenney heal. What the sergeant appreciated most from this organization was that the counselors were veterans themselves and thus could relate to his specific needs. After all, they spoke the same warrior language and wore the same familiar fatigues.

I originally met Sgt. Kenney at an air show. While sporting a large frame and a huge smile, he didn't seem like a tough army soldier with a few combat tours under his belt. Sgt. Kenney's life has a different meaning as a civilian. He's a brave man indeed, for his new job involves being part of the solution of helping veterans suffering with PTSD. This unique team puts veterans with veterans so they can discuss their problems, and it helps these warriors get jobs. Sgt. Kenney explained to me that many vets lose hope and become homeless. Sgt. Kenney helps homeless veterans get back on their feet. From contemplating suicide to reaching out and helping vets, Sgt. Kenney and Ann are heroes in my book! Thank you, Sgt. Kenney, for your service and example as an amazing man. May God continue to bless and guide you as you use your unique life history to better the lives of America's warriors.

Sgt. Kenney told me that Psalm 139:5–7 showed him how David recognized that God was with him no matter what:

> You hem me in behind and before, and you lay your
> hand upon me.

> *Such knowledge is too wonderful for me, too lofty for*
> *me to attain.*
> *Where can I go from your Spirit? Where can I flee*
> *from your presence?*

It was hard for David to fathom, but it was true nonetheless. Sgt. Kenney also shared "that Jesus is with us every step of the way through the good and bad times, but it is hard for us to realize that truth." Well, it is true. God does reign and He loves you. Never give up hope. Trust in the Lord in all ways. America needs you still, as do many hurting veterans returning from the war zone.

If you're not a veteran and wish to help, please consider supporting Operation Finally Home, the PTSD Foundation of America, or DNA Military. There are many good people working to help veterans. They need your prayers, time, and financial support. If you are a businessperson, hire veterans, especially those wounded while serving. These warriors have hearts of lions. They are courageous in battle. Loyal. Disciplined. Men and women of honor. Give them a shot and help them be productive and part of your team. You need them more than they need you.

America, never forget these amazing people. Honor them and their sacrifices. The souls of the wounded cry out for help. Next time you see a homeless person who is a veteran, consider his cries for help. Lend a hand. Go the extra mile to connect him with local churches or veteran groups. Finally, never forget those who have paid the ultimate sacrifice with their lives in defense of our freedom. They are amazing men and women indeed.

Lord God, You alone know the scars we warriors have faced, and we ask that You heal us. Use our war experiences to be a source of good and healing to others needing help.

DO YOU KNOW OF ANY AMAZING WARRIORS suffering from PTSD? How can you lend a helping hand and a listening ear? What credible organizations do you know of where you could volunteer time or money? Check out the appendixes or log on to www.calledtoserveministry.com and click "Support a Warrior" to get ideas of how you can serve those who serve our country.

Resources

See appendix B for thoroughly reviewed combat-related stress helps.

SEVENTEEN

Everyone Needs an Angela

Encouraging Others

A word fitly spoken is like apples of gold in a setting of silver.

Proverbs 25:11,
English Standard Version

I stood in the restroom line with twenty-some fellow passengers after landing in Atlanta for a book convention. As I waited, I watched a woman in a yellow uniform struggling to scrub the toilets. Her heavy sighs expressed frustration as the influx of travelers kept interrupting her cleaning of the individual stalls. This process reminded me of when I was a child on the beach and would run to gather a wanted seashell from the shoreline before the next wave rushed in, grabbing it from my grasp.

I excused myself as I wheeled my luggage past her into the neighboring stall and then again as I passed her while exiting through a growing line of waiting travelers. As I headed toward the baggage claim, I abruptly stopped. I thought of Angela and U-turned back into the restroom, bypassing the newly formed line of women, who probably thought, *Who does she think she is, cutting in line?* Or *Boy, she* really *has to go!* I poked my head into the stall where the woman briskly scrubbed the commode and said, "Thank you so much for what you are doing. A clean restroom is so nice after a long trip." The woman looked at me as if my neck held three heads, but regardless of her surprised response, her demeanor changed. As I left, she hummed happily.

Thanks, Angela, I said to myself and smiled inside. Just one kind word can change another's day.

Angela, who was seventy-two years old when we first met, taught me this golden lesson of encouraging others, along with many other golden nuggets of wisdom too numerous to count. The first time I met the smiling, five-foot-tall powerhouse of praise, she grabbed my hands and cupped them into her own. While looking into my eyes with a gaze that would melt a superhero's power, she said, "Aren't you the sweetest little thing." I thought, *I'm going to really like this new church,* as we settled into our seats in the small Missouri town that we would call home until military orders decided otherwise. I was unaware that I had just met my new best friend and my mentor for the next sixteen years. This petite woman who was nearly twice my age had not just touched my hands. She would touch my heart as well.

Angela soon became my die-hard encourager. The lessons learned were more priceless than any book ever written, any Dr. Phil show ever aired, or any self-help course ever produced. Angela taught me to see the beauty in *all* people, to never judge, to listen rather than speak, to laugh often, and not to take life so seriously or for granted. She taught me how to love my husband, seek God's direction over my own, encourage others, and discover the limitless power contained in just a few words aptly spoken.

A few months after her husband, Virgil, went home to the Lord, I asked Angela to accompany me on a road trip to my dad's home in Arkansas. Along the eight-hour drive, nature called. We had trouble finding a rest area in the Ozark Mountains' back roads, but finally we approached a small-town service station. You know the kind, the one where the employee hands you an ironing-board-sized plank attached to the bathroom key so you don't accidentally leave with it. As I opened the wobbly lock, a young man with a hole in his earlobe big enough to see my car through it approached with a young woman. I wondered if the two of them possessed magnetic powers and had just visited a scrap metal shop. Numerous silver shapes pierced their noses, lips, tongues, eyebrows, and cheeks. Tattoos blanketed nearly all their exposed skin. I quickly whispered to Angela, "I'll let them go first." She replied with a wink, "No, Honey. You go before you soak your pants, and I have to drive with my head out the window. I'll be just fine." She then prodded me into the restroom. I never went to the bathroom so fast.

When I opened the door, Angela and the waiting couple were laughing like old friends. Angela explained to me that they were engaged, and the girl, Elise, was already having in-law problems. Angela and Elise exchanged phone numbers before we left. Angela attracted people of every background, ethnicity, and age through her encouraging personality.

Several months after our trip, Angela became increasingly confused and was diagnosed with Alzheimer's disease. My role of friend transformed overnight into caregiver since her children lived out of state. For several months, I visited her, prepared meals, and administered medication. Even while she grieved for Virgil and recognized that her mind was not right, Angela never complained. She continuously focused on her blessings and encouraged everyone she came in contact with.

One day I walked into her home and found her crying; she was panicked and lost in her own home. Living alone had become unsafe. Her daughter arranged admittance into a peaceful assisted-living facility near her many friends. We communicated nearly every day, and I picked her up or visited her weekly at her homey apartment. During those visits, I learned that she had bedazzled the entire staff with her charm. No matter where Angela dwelled, she continuously encouraged. She may have praised others with the same compliments over and over, but who gets tired of hearing, "You've lost weight" or "That blouse makes your beautiful blue eyes sparkle"?

One day I called to tell her that I was on my way to visit. Angela said that she was not up for visitors. Something was gravely wrong. Angela never turned away friends no matter how tired she felt. I went to her apartment anyway. Angela did not have strength to get out of bed. Her daughter immediately responded and arrived the next day. After Angela received her cancer diagnosis, we expressed our feelings. She reassured, "Penny, I am perfectly all right with this." I replied in a choked voice, "I know, Angela, but I'm going to miss you terribly!" She looked at me sternly and scolded me while smiling her infectious smile, "Honey, now you know that we're going to see each other again!" and that was that. Angela encouraged until her voice was too weak to speak.

Within one week of her diagnosis, she joined her Father in heaven along with her beloved Virgil. She and I used to joke about how Virgil undoubtedly headed God's gardening committee, exhausting the angels with meticulous instructions on how to landscape heaven. Now I envisioned Angela passing out lemonade to each gardening angel, praising how good their halos looked while waving to Virgil on his riding lawn mower.

Life on this earth can be tough, but when you surround yourself with positiveness, especially while undergoing challenges, trying situations become much more tolerable. If you currently lack a godly mentor, pray for one to grace your life. Find one who will stand by your side when life's stress overwhelms you, pray for you, and rejoice in your victories. Filter your life from discouraging news, pessimistic people, and movies and books whose morals make a toilet bowl look clean.

You have mentors in your midst. They share the pews in your church. They have traveled through circumstances where you knowingly or unknowingly are going, and they can tell you exactly what to pack, what the weather will be like when you arrive, what kind of people you will run into, and most importantly, how to enjoy the journey.

If you are a "seasoned" Christian who feels that God has already fulfilled your life's purpose, then let these words assure you: There is work to be done! Look around. You have boatloads of younger men and women who feel they are drowning from life's pressures. They are in over their heads, and you may be the only one in their path holding a life preserver. They face military, parenting, and life challenges. Share your wisdom and the hope you have in Christ. Be the Angela to our younger men and women who so desperately need spiritual guidance to travel the roads you have already traveled so they can enjoy the journey.

Encouragement only takes a moment and can be displayed in numerous ways, but its effects ripple beyond one's life span to transcend generations. I see the positive effects of military warriors, parents, and family members mentoring each other daily on Facebook's military forums. I couldn't hold back the tears as I read the encouraging post from a Chicago mom whose words reached across cyberspace to hug a distraught blue star mom in Houston whose son just deployed into the combat zone.[12] Tips on child rearing and recipes are shared. Spouses market their home-based businesses to provide additional family income. Frustration over broken household goods and other military challenges are vented. By the last comment posted, the stress has been diffused, humorous stories are

---

12. Mothers of active duty warriors or veterans are called "blue star moms." The Blue Star Flag was designed during World War I. Each star on the flag represents how many living children currently serve or have served in the US Armed Forces. The flags are hung in household windows, signifying the love, pride, and hope for children serving in war. If the service member's life is sacrificed for America, the blue star changes to gold.

shared, and friendships between strangers have been forged. When a military parent grieves over the loss of their fallen warrior, the entire military Internet community drops to their knees in prayer and carries their pain.

We need encouragement and mentors like Angela, especially while we are separated by distance from our families. Support from family, friends, and mentors is crucial so that you don't travel the hills and valleys alone. More importantly, we need to be an Angela to others needing encouragement. Just a few aptly spoken words can change another's day and positively impact their life.

Dear Lord, help me find a godly mentor to keep me centered on life's blessings and to provide wisdom for life's challenges. Place people in my life today that I can be an "Angela" to and inspire them with the hope that comes from knowing You.

HOW ARE YOU CURRENTLY enriching your life with positive influences? What person can you call on for godly wisdom? Does your church provide a mentoring group? If not, why not create one?

Resources

Here are some online support sites that are just drops in the deep well of mentoring support. Through these sites, the entire military community resounds with "We are in this together." Search on Facebook under "military" and you will discover numerous groups for every branch of service and every aspect of military life. Here are some sites where I found a display of great encouragement from fellow spouses and military parents:

Air Force Moms Support
Called to Serve: Strength for Military Families and
  Those Who Love Them (a personal favorite)
Deployment: One Day at a Time
Diapers and Deployments
Military Moms of Texas
Military Wives Businesses
My Heart Deployed
Parents of Fallen Heroes
Proud and Strong Army Moms-Hooah
Proud Marine Parents
PTSD Support
Support Our Troops
Wounded Warrior Spouses

PART 4

Reintegration

EIGHTEEN

Take the High Ground

Maintaining Character During Relationship Challenges

That is why, for Christ's sake, I delight in weaknesses, in insults, in hardships, in persecutions, in difficulties. For when I am weak, then I am strong.

2 Corinthians 12:10

"The huge greenhouse around the corner is on fire!" shouted my teenage friend Mike as he skidded into my driveway with his bicycle. Within seconds, I was on my bike checking out the burning house surrounded by firefighters. Wailing fire truck sirens, the smell of smoke, and the sensation of the heat emanating from the fire overwhelmed my senses. I was mesmerized by the destruction and state of confusion. Within minutes, flames were shooting up through the windows, and the fire was out of control. What was once an old Victorian home now resembled a huge barn fire, as the flames and ashes rose high into the night sky. Luckily, no one was in the building, and it appeared that the firefighters were spraying the surrounding areas, having given up on saving the house. The once proud home was consumed by fire, and eventually only the foundation remained.

I thought of that sight when I looked into the eyes of a fellow airman who lost his family through divorce. His wife of over fifteen years had an alleged illicit affair, and their once tight Christian family was enduring litigation and custody hearings. He had been oblivious to the fact that his wife was having an affair and within months, the marriage was over. The divorce papers were signed the day I coincidentally walked into his office. He was now a single man, while his former spouse took primary custody of the children, possession of their home, and half his salary. I could tell that this fellow airman and friend was hurting inside, and my heart ached for him and his family as he opened up to me about the divorce and its ugly consequences.

While he shared his point of view and feelings, I prayed for guidance. The words poured out. "Take the high ground," I responded, "and be a man of character and honor during this tough time." He explained that the harsh words were already spoken and the custody battle was over. But I reminded him that nothing was over, for we still have today and tomorrow to look forward to.

"Do not speak ill against your ex-wife to anyone," I said. "Forgive her. Stand for truth, and don't take part in any further destructive talk, otherwise bitterness will take hold and make things worse for you and your family." The Bible verse "for when I am weak then I am strong" (2 Corinthians 12:10) echoed in my mind as I spoke with him. I sensed that he yearned for someone to listen to his ordeal and for me to stay. I recommended he take refuge in knowing that

God's Word is truth and could be depended upon always, especially during times of trials. I continued, "Although you may never be able to forget the suffering she caused, take the high ground. Rely on Jesus Christ for comfort, and cling to his love and example in your time of need." When Jesus was persecuted by those around Him and abandoned by most of His disciples when sent to the cross, He relied on God to get Him through the suffering."

While standing there, I asked if we could pray together, and he gladly accepted. I put my arm around his shoulders and prayed with him. My prayer pertains to you too, if you are facing similar challenges. May you have wisdom and strength during this time of need, and may God lift you up so you have the courage and strength to take the high ground. Then, someday, after the flames are put out, the smoke is gone, and the debris is removed, that new hope can be built on the firm foundation of love that comes through Christ. Follow Jesus' positive example of trusting in God, and someday, all will know the truth for what it is.

Tragedy does and will strike, for that's life. But we can take courage in knowing that a powerful God exists. By relying on His love, you'll be strengthened during your fires and lifted up above the smoke. God will never abandon you during your time of need. He may not extinguish all fires in your preferred timetable, or perhaps even your lifetime, but when the dust settles and the smoke clears, your foundation will remain strong in the hope and strength that comes from the love of God.

If you're a warrior or spouse who has experienced broken relationships that deeply wounded you, I encourage you to continue praying to God for guidance and find friends and family for support. Seek help from counselors who are trained for this season of crisis, and don't tackle it alone. Resist the temptation of speaking ill of the person you once shared a sacred vow or trust with, especially to your children and immediate family. Do your very best to maintain personal dignity. Avoid using alcohol or drugs to numb the pain. Nothing good ever comes from that. If you're feeling hopeless, even suicidal, please seek help and know that you're needed and loved.

Remember most of all that the person who wounded you cannot take away your happiness, for that comes from within. It's hard seeing that when you're in the raging flames of a marital fire. I can relate, for I went through a relationship fire with my wife, Penny, and I felt hopeless. I felt so lost because I thought the love we once shared was gone. I recall only seeing emptiness when looking into her eyes. But I took hope in believing that with God all things are possible (Matthew 19:26), and I stood firm on my foundation of Christ. Through his love and the help of counselors, family, and friends, we made it through the fire. Thankfully, my story ended in a saved marriage, but that's not always the case.

Prior to seeking counseling, I resorted to drinking alcohol. That was the worst thing I could do, for it led me to say things to my family that I later regretted. It has taken years to rebuild our marriage and family, but the sacrifice has been well worth it. If you're going through a similar relationship problem, first let me express how sorry I am for your pain, but take courage in knowing that you are not alone. There are many good people and trained counselors and chaplains who want to help. There are family members who love you and need you. Most importantly, know that God loves you. Our hope resides in this foundation. And His love is available to all who will humble themselves to the power and love of God. The fires of life will come, but the foundation built on God's love will not crumble. For when you are weak, then you too, will be made strong!

Heavenly Father, during my times of tragedy, when all seems lost, remind me to focus on Christ and lift me up above the flames. Use me to lift others up and to take the high ground when I would rather strike back.

DO YOU KNOW OF SOMEONE who is hurting and needing a friend? What will happen to that person if you do nothing? Are you consumed by fire and overwhelmed with despair? What positive actions are you taking to lessen the pain? What foundation are you standing on?

NINETEEN

Getting Rid of Land Mines!

Transitioning Home

I am with you and will watch over you wherever you go,
and I will bring you back to this land.

Genesis 28:15

"Where are you going?"

"Outside."

"What's the matter?"

"There's a bunch of dog poop out there."

"AND?"

"I need to pick it up."

"For real? Are you serious? You're going to clean the backyard now of all times?"

"Yup," Tony answered.

I stared in disbelief.

Rewind several days. I had finally allowed myself to be hopeful for Tony's homecoming after being separated because of an open-ended deployment. Not only was his destination unknown when he told me he was leaving, but I also had no anticipated day of his return. Now, after months of separation, the 668th Bomb Squadron spouses received the awaited notification of their warriors' return. They would land in ten days!

When the homecoming was finally announced, I excitedly prepared. I called my family and my relieved Italian in-laws, who immediately planned a big Brooklyn homecoming party. Whenever they get excited, they revert to their native Italian language, so I only understood half of what they were saying. I bought ingredients for Tony's favorite dinner, spaghetti and clams, and a homemade cake (not the kind out of a box). My two-year-old son, Nico, and I colored and hung homemade "Welcome Home" posters. Then, two days before Tony's expected arrival, the commander called. Tony's crew was being delayed for one week. After months of waiting for his return, what was seven more days, right? I donated the cake to a church function, called my family, and drove to a friend's house since her husband was detained also. We commiserated together but soon began re-making homecoming plans.

As I baked another cake the day before Tony's re-scheduled arrival, the phone rang. For the first time, I hoped that an annoying telemarketer was calling to offer a vacation timeshare. But it was Tony's commander. "Have you heard the news yet?" he asked.

I replied, "I won a trip to the Bahamas?"

Confused, he ignored my attempt at humor. "The crew's plane has maintenance problems. When the part arrives, they will take off—if all goes well—in three days, but it could take up to ten more days."

Disheartened, I called my family to once again squash their home-coming joy. This bad-news-bearing Betty Crocker was becoming burned out. After explaining in two-year-old lingo that Daddy was not coming home *again* because his plane broke, I escaped to another room not to upset Nico by my tears. However, after he offered me his glue to fix Daddy's plane, I couldn't help but laugh. After that second phone call, I lowered my expectations for when Tony was to arrive, but I soon discovered that my expectations should have changed after his return as well.

The call announcing that the B-52 was airborne finally arrived, and Tony's crew anticipated landing in seven hours. As the home-coming hour neared, I changed into my American flag sweater, found the mini flags for Nico to wave, and headed to the airfield. Eager spouses and their children lined the tarmac, holding patriotic posters and gigantic yellow ribbons. The electrifying enthusiasm could have powered New York City. Then the distant roar of engines announced the B-52's approach as we watched the sky fill with the gigantic plane, elevating our excitement even higher. Two airmen stood on a military van's roof, waving a ten-foot flag. Red, white, and blue would be the B-52 crew's first welcoming vision as they set eyes on their homeland. Nico frantically waved his mini flags so his daddy would know where to land his "co-plane." The long-awaited homecoming was actually happening!

The last pair of boots descending the plane's ladder was attached to my tan, physically fit, ten-pounds-thinner-than-before-he-left husband. The rope corralling the anxious spouses lifted. Nico and I dashed toward Tony, leaping into his embrace. There we were—together—a complete family again. That momentous day lives in my heart forever. After all the worry, the loneliness, the true stories, and the rampant rumors about dangerous missions that infected and spread throughout the spouse's network like a virus, it was going to be fine now. At least, that's what I thought!

After returning to our base duplex, I laid my over-tired son down for a nap. Tony and I were alone. I waited for his embrace as he glanced out the window. Instead, he stood up, walked to the back door, and exited into our fenced-in yard. Confused, I questioned, "Where are you going?"

"Outside."

"What's the matter?"

"There's a bunch of dog poop outside."

So, there we were. After months of homecoming anticipation, my husband preferred to pick up dog doo-doo than spend time alone with me. We owned a 120-pound Rottweiler. While preparing the homecoming celebration inside, I forgot about the elephant-sized land mines decorating our yard outside. When Tony headed to the backyard, my emotions summersaulted. *Why in the world was he not holding me? No person, book, or informational deployment meeting warned me this might happen! Does he love me as much as he used to? Does he still find me attractive?* The negative thoughts bombarded my brain. *Did he meet someone while defending our country? Was that even a possibility?* Then the bunk buddy to my negative emotions, guilt, jumped into the mental boxing ring. *What a terrible wife you are! How can you think such awful thoughts when your husband has been risking his life? You should be ashamed, and don't even think of asking such offensive questions!*

My mind ping-ponged the conflicting thoughts. Seeing Tony in the backyard caused our duplex neighbors to naturally conclude that our alone time was over. The cheering "Welcome homes" outside my napping son's window woke up a terribly cranky child. My homecoming expectations were shattered, but how could I be so selfish to feel hurt? My husband had just returned home from combat.

Discussing the foiled homecoming healed my hurt as we sorted through our initial emotions. I learned that jumping back into the husband and dad role after deploying made Tony apprehensive. The dog poop, of all things, was an outlet for more time to adjust. His stress level remained in the combat zone although he safely walked on American soil. I envisioned hugs and tenderness. Tony had to adjust from dropping bombs in the combat zone to dropping off mail at the post office.

The dog piles outside signified that many veterans carry mental land mines, which stink up their normal thought process. I discovered great lessons during that first homecoming: Lower your expectations after a spouse, son, or daughter returns from combat, patiently allow time to readjust, and educate yourself about transitioning from the combat zone to the home front so you can better understand their challenges.

Before a warrior first returns, explain to family members the need for a gradual reintegration into social activities. Save the Disney trip or huge family reunion until after the initial transition period, which varies for each combat veteran from a couple of days to weeks or more. Communicate with your warrior about his homecoming wishes and remain open-minded when those desires do not parallel your plans.

After a warrior leaves the combat zone and returns to America's safety, his adrenal valve may remain stuck in the "on" position. Warriors are trained to react opposite of the brain's natural instinct to flee *from* danger. Instead, the warrior charges *toward* the threat. Warriors become accustomed to increased adrenal levels triggered by experiencing or witnessing traumatic events and heightened stress. This constant war-induced adrenal surge inhibits the endocrine system from performing efficiently. Many returning veterans indulge in "adrenaline chasing," thrill-seeking activities that may contradict their pre-deployment character. These are attempts to match war's intensity, which is impossible.

Many returning veterans purchase motorcycles to fill this need. More marines were killed in 2008 by motorcycles than by insurgent groups in Iraq.[13] Some soldiers call it "legal crack cocaine," suggesting that the bike fills the adrenaline void left behind in the war zone.[14] Motorcycle fatality rates increase during the three-to-nine month period after veterans return from deployment, and the risk of death from a motor-vehicle accident is much higher during the first five years after redeployment, regardless of gender. [15]

Post-traumatic stress disorder (PTSD) and traumatic brain injury (TBI) symptoms may take months, even years, to surface. This is why

13. Nicholas D. Kristof, "A Veteran's Death, the Nation's Shame," New York Times Sunday Review, *New York Times*, 14 April 2012.

14. Biker Red, "Returning Troops Face New Dangers on American Roads," Russ Brown.com, 14 March 2012.

15. Captain John R. Beal, "Ban the Bike—Should the Marine Corp Ban Motorcycles?" *Marine Corps Gazette*, 16 July 2010; and Staff Sgt. Michael J. Carden, "Departments Launch Safe-Driving Initiative for Veterans," US Department of Defense, 12 January 2009.

it's so important to become educated about combat-related stress. If you are a spouse or parent and notice that your warrior is experiencing post-traumatic stress (PTS), also known as operational combat stress (OCS), that has lasted more than a month and that interferes with daily life, don't hesitate to seek help. First, realize that the warrior's behavior and your responses are normal reactions to an abnormal situation and that you are not alone. Please also take time to read appendix B, "Combat-Related Stress Helps."

It took patience waiting for Tony to readjust to family life. Warriors will be changed by combat for life. However, educating yourself to understand your warrior's coping mechanisms means you are on the road to recovery. Explore coping and communication techniques to forge an even closer relationship than before the warrior deployed. Include the entire family in the restoration process, and invite God to lead this initiative.

Several weeks after the homecoming, Tony looked out the back window at the yard. A blizzard had prevented us from deactivating the canine land mines. Tony called to me as I prepared dinner and asked me to join him on the couch. He closed the curtains, and said, "I'll get those later. It's good to be home," and then he hugged me tenderly.

Dear Lord, strengthen us on our journey to restore intimacy and communication in our relationships and lives. Remove the land mines that pollute our minds, which could stem from combat or just everyday stresses. Give us courage to seek professional help, and renew our faith daily. Thank You for being our ultimate healer and assuring us that nothing is impossible for you.

ARE YOU OR SOMEONE YOU KNOW living with combat stress? What steps are you taking before, during, and after to educate yourself about PTSD? How can you minister to a fellow warrior or family member who is battling the invisible wounds of war?

Resources

Check out appendix B, "Combat-Related Stress Helps," for thoroughly reviewed resources to assist warriors and family members challenged with combat stress, and visit www.calledtoserveministry.com for additional support.

TWENTY

It's Okay to Say No

Protecting Our Children

Children, obey your parents in everything, for this pleases the Lord. Fathers, do not provoke your children, lest they become discouraged.

Colossians 3:20–21,
English Standard Version

The crowded bleachers were filled with proud parents eagerly awaiting the graduation ceremony of America's newest army soldiers on the parade fields of Fort Jackson, South Carolina. My son, Antonio, was out there somewhere.

Four years earlier, I had hosted a team of Army Special Forces as they tested base security systems. These combat-tested "snake eaters"[16] were the real deal, and Antonio was ecstatic to meet them, for his childhood dream was to be an army soldier. After the team

---

16. A military term denoting special forces.

enjoyed our home-cooked meal, I asked them if they had advice for my army wannabe son, who at the time was a high school freshman. Each officer suggested Antonio enlist in the army, become a soldier first, and then earn the rank of officer, if he chose to. Their united response took me off guard, as I thought it would be better for Antonio to attend college first. Antonio grinned from ear to ear, and the rest is history.

While caught up in the sea of emotions and wondering what would be next for my son as an enlisted army soldier volunteering during a time of war, I realized some of the things I did right and some of the things that I need to improve on as a father. For the most part, I tried saying "yes" more than saying "no" when raising my children, but there were certain things that I stood firm on. I was against their sleeping over at other people's homes, for example. It was my belief that you never know what may happen under someone else's roof. However, we encouraged our children to have friend sleepovers at our home regularly. I encouraged them to say no to drugs and racism. Finding the proper balance on how much time to spend at work was always a challenge for me. It comes down to knowing what you value most and then making wise choices. My commitment to my nation was strong, but I prioritized God, family, and then profession. I always did my best to encourage my children to live their dreams and to go for it. I was perhaps a bit too demanding.

Having children is an awesome responsibility, and raising them is a challenge. The Old and New Testaments are clear that we should discipline our children yet not discourage them. How we go about disciplining them is a challenge, and each parent has ideas as to what works best.

My parents served as great role models. They adhered to certain rules that I hated at the time but now understand. Even though my parents devoted their lives to protecting me, I experienced my share of close encounters with evil people growing up in New York City. One particular event rocked my world. As a teenager, I was awarded the New York City Mayor Young Leadership Medal. After receiving the award from Mayor Ed Koch and after the bleachers cleared from the outdoor ceremony at city hall, the devil incarnate approached me. I just didn't recognize it at the time.

His name was Tom. He introduced himself as the president of the New York Young Republican Club and offered me the opportunity to be part of this prestigious organization. Tom appeared to be a jovial, educated man, and he invited me to see his law office in New York City. I was impressed that he took an interest in me. He enthusiastically shared a vision for my future, one involving politics. I explained that my interests were in serving in the military as an Air Force pilot more than anything else. Tom explained a different viewpoint, suggesting that I could use my leadership skills through the New York Young Republican Club organization. In fact, he was hosting a convention at a Staten Island hotel and invited me as his special guest. My parents were against me sleeping anywhere but in my home, but I assured them that Tom was a good guy. After all, he was a respected attorney and president of this prestigious club. My mother had an instinct that I shouldn't go, but I was able to persuade my family to allow me to attend.

When we arrived at the hotel, I asked where the conference was being held. He told me to go to his hotel room first to prepare for the event. While in his room, he gave me orange juice, but I sensed that something was seriously wrong when I began feeling strange. Because of my suspicion, I spilled the remainder of the drink onto the carpet. I became confused, and before I knew it, he had disrobed me. When I realized that he was taking pictures, I faked being severely sick and managed to convince him to call an ambulance.

There's much more to this story, but by the grace of God, he was unable to accomplish all of his evil plans. Tom vowed to never contact me again, and I have not seen him since that hellish night. I was concerned what others might think and embarrassed that I wasn't able to prevent the events from happening. I never told anyone until recently. To this day, I cringe at the thought that this monster preyed on other unsuspecting victims because of my silence, and it's my prayer that justice will be served, in this life or the next. I thanked God for protecting me as I walked home from the Verrazano Bridge that evening, back to the safety of the Monetti household.

As a teenager, my home was my refuge. The dinner table, especially, was a sanctuary where we could say anything. One evening, I was excited to share with my family that my friends and I were getting tattoos. On my right calf I planned to design an eagle grasping a United States flag. My mom's "wadda you crazy?" look on her face conveyed that she didn't share my enthusiasm. My dad, while sitting at the head of the table, remarkably showed no change in disposition. He kept eating. When I finished explaining my intentions, he simply pushed his chair back from the table, wiped his lips with his napkin, looked me in the eyes, and calmly stated, "Okay, Son, go ahead, get your tattoo. But tomorrow night after dinner, I will take it off!" He then asked for more pasta and proceeded with his meal. I didn't get a tattoo, nor did any of my friends for that matter. Looking back, I'm glad my dad laid down the law and set boundaries. There are indeed times to say "no."

As I was growing up in Brooklyn, New York, drugs and gangs were rampant. I never tried drugs, mainly because of my mother. She sacrificed having a career to be a stay-at-home mom, and she always embraced us with love, stability, and awesome food. She strongly emphasized that if we ever did drugs, it would kill her. One evening while I was "hanging out" under the train station near Café Aurora, a local drug dealer known as "Little Anthony" offered my friends and me free drugs. When I refused, he made fun of me and chided, "What's the matter, you too cool for us? From here on out, your name is Cool Breeze." The primary reason I didn't try drugs was for my mom. Her simple message resonated and gave me the courage to say no. I loved my mom so much that I didn't want to hurt her, let alone be responsible for her death.

Military children deal with greater challenges than most peers their age, due to the numerous moves that military life demands. My oldest son attended six different middle schools and high schools due to military orders. If not raised with love and discipline, children may indulge in risky behaviors to gain acceptance by peers.

If you're a parent, be sincere with your children. Let them know that you're doing your best while serving our country, and show them through your actions and words that you value and love them.

Our military service may not allow us to attend many of their programs, activities, or "firsts," so prioritize quality time with your children when you are at home.

If you behave as a militant control freak at home, then change your ways. I'm especially talking to dads. If you act tough and rigid at home, it'll likely result in alienating and discouraging your children. Some fathers unknowingly discourage their kids for not meeting their high standards. Your kids will not respect you if you're so demanding all the time, and they may rebel. It's okay to say "no" and set boundaries, but do so with love and understanding. My dad threatening to take off my tattoo worked for me. I knew he was joking. Well, sort of. My parents advising me to avoid gangs and drugs prepared me for the real world. My pushing my parents to allow me to spend time with a man they were unsure of was wrong.

After raising three wonderful children, my recommendations are to avoid being brash, especially with teenage girls. I found that when I raise my voice to my daughter, it affects her much more than my sons. Discipline out of love and do so in a way that will not alienate your child. Leave work at work and remember that children are not recruits. I've learned many of these lessons the hard way. The Scriptures are clear that children should obey their parents and that fathers should not provoke their children: "Children, obey your parents in the Lord, for this is right. . . . Fathers, do not exasperate your children; instead, bring them up in the training and instruction of the Lord" (Ephesians 6:1, 4). Notice that the command is directed to fathers.

There are times to say "yes" and times to say "no." Give prior thought to saying no, and encourage children to make wise choices.

Better they learn now while you can influence them. Before you know it, your child will be standing on a parade field, or you'll be watching your offspring board a plane to begin his or her own life adventure. Cherish your time with your family and give them all you've got. Encourage them to live their dreams. Life is rich when you realize that your life has meaning, and what can be more fulfilling than knowing that you did your best raising your family to face life's challenges with strength, honor, and faith, while doing everything you could to shield them from the evils in this world.

Heavenly Father, protect my children from evil and give me wisdom on how to best raise them. Send guardian angels to surround them and shield them from evil. Help my children to make wise choices.

FATHERS, HOW DO YOU SPEND TIME with your children? Are you doing activities together that interest them or you? What areas need strengthening in your relationship with your children? How well do you know them? What are the names of your child's stuffed animals? What are the names of your child's friends? What are your child's dreams?

TWENTY-ONE

From Down Range to Delta Phi

Attending College After Combat

Let us not give up meeting together, as some are in the habit of doing, but let us encourage one another.

Hebrews 10:25,
NIV (1984)

"Would you like to cater for our veterans' group at the university?" The tanned, fit, twentysomething man asked me this question as he sat alone at the round-top table for two at our Italian pizzeria. "Sure! We love veterans." When I shared that I give presentations to military groups regarding their unique challenges such as transitions, combat-related stress, and stress on marriages, the communication floodgates opened. We had recently recommitted our little Italian pizzeria, just a few blocks from the university, to God, and He wasted no time leading Joe, an army veteran harboring invisible wounds, through the doors. The expected dinner crowd would soon fill the empty tables. I prayed that God would fill Joe's heart with hope, as well.

"I've been a soldier for six years and deployed four times. Walking out on my marriage was easier than sorting it out," he confessed.

"You're not alone," I reassured him. "Many warriors don't know how to turn off the combat zone and turn on family life, but there is a transition and healing process; however, it takes commitment, education, and patience from both partners."

Joe replied, "The military gives mandatory debriefs when we return from deployments before we reconnect with our families, but if we check the box admitting we have post-traumatic stress symptoms, we are retained for counseling, and we have to postpone seeing our families. Who wants to do that after a year of separation? Nobody checks that box. Besides, many of us experience stress symptoms months *after* we return to the civilian world. Lots of veterans, like me, get out of the military and enroll into college with their GI Bill. While we're still processing what we've seen in combat, we're thrown into the mix of students whose biggest concern is if they got the class they wanted or finding a party's address. A common question they ask when they find out I'm a veteran is, 'Have you killed anyone or seen someone die?' They don't understand the pain that causes inside, so now I don't tell anyone I'm a veteran. I can't read history assignments about war, because I immediately relive Afghanistan. My brother returned from combat, and after one year, he took his life. I'm not missing a leg, so nobody can see my injuries, but every day is a struggle to live."

At that moment, I realized the harsh challenge veterans face when transitioning from the combat zone to civilian and campus life. Currently over 800,000 military men and women are enrolled in higher education using the post–9/11 GI Bill, and that does not include those veterans and service members using other financial sources to obtain their chosen credential.[17] As the military continues to draw down its forces overseas and active and reserve units return stateside, thousands more veterans will reintegrate into the civilian realm. Campuses nationwide are experiencing an influx of military students. Transitioning from combat to the college campus and civilian life is complex. Veterans need help for combat-related stress and don't know where to turn.

There are two cutting-edge universities whose innovative reintegration programs are setting skyscraping standards for campuses nationwide to emulate. If you are affiliated with a university, does your institution have a student veterans' center and not just a VA office that assists processing tuition from a GI Bill? If not, perhaps introducing the following ideas to your educational institution is how you can help. The following schools not only assist veterans transitioning into the classroom, but they also reach across the educational perimeters to provide healing for the invisible wounds of war.

One such beacon of hope is the University of Central Missouri (UCM) in Warrensburg, Missouri. Its second-to-none Military Veteran Success Center (MVSC) provides a location for military students to bond with fellow veterans experiencing the same challenges. Many veterans attest that the friendships forged through war are stronger than family bonds. A warrior will sacrifice his own life to protect a friend while in combat and vice versa. Fitting in with

---

17. Dr. Randy Plunkett, "Student Veterans of America: A Needed Resource," *Military.com Education*, Military Advantage, 2012.

students who have no concept of the war zone is frustrating. At UCM's MVSC, veterans directly access a dedicated staff that knows military challenges firsthand. UCM's leadership understands the gravity of veteran mentorship and positioned a decorated Vietnam war veteran and Purple Heart recipient, Charles "Lynn" Lowder, as the director of Military and Veteran Services.

When asked how the MVSC's programs are unique, Lowder passionately replied, "Our program is not just *good* for those that served in combat, it's *ideal*." He uses three S's to describe the program's authenticity. "It's safe, secure, and supportive. Here veterans get themselves centered. The MVSC is a clubhouse for veterans where friendships form and healing takes place. Many universities labeled as 'military friendly' set up programs where the office resides in a dorm room. What message of value does that send to a veteran? Then someone from an administration department is thrown into a position to head the veterans' program. Regardless of their great intentions, they have no combat experience. The military is relational and honor driven; it is all about trust. Leadership from one who has *been there and done that* solidifies that trust."

The "been there and done that" theme flows over into the success center's coping and healing opportunities for veterans challenged by operational combat stress (OCS) and post-traumatic stress disorder (PTSD). Mental health is monumental at UCM. The Kansas City VA holds weekly therapy sessions on campus. A short-term referral system allows immediate help for veterans. Delilah Nichols, the MVSC service coordinator, stated, "The road to healing is tough, but once a veteran *chooses* to get better, *nothing* can stop him, but he has to make that choice. We help veterans travel the road so they are not alone; we are available 24/7." Future plans include a full-time counselor located inside the center and post-traumatic stress awareness training for faculty members.

Another monumental challenge veterans face is post-education employment. UCM is establishing a full-service career center. Instead of giving lip service to being veteran friendly, UCM focuses on job placement and deals only with companies that are sincere about placing veterans. UCM also recognizes the sacrifices female warriors make and address their unique challenges at conferences. Unlike most campuses, UCM's services now encompass National Guardsmen as well.

Lowder concluded, "God has a special place in His heart for the warrior who stands in the gap. 'Greater love has no man that will lay down his life for a friend.' There is something so righteous about our warriors. The Lord loves justice, and veterans have been treated unjustly in the past. I left this country for three years after Vietnam because of the brutal ways veterans were treated. UCM focuses on justice and respect for our veterans. The military community is all about doing. As far as I'm concerned, colleges need to stop talking and start doing. If our programs encourage just one veteran to get on with his life, our efforts will be worth it. But we're going to do better than one!"

Another school that demonstrates world-class veteran assistance is Liberty University's (LU) Institute of Military Resiliency (IMR). This ingenious program at the Lynchburg, Virginia, school offers exceptional, accredited online and campus courses not only for veterans battling post-traumatic stress but also for their spouses, parents, pastors, and friends. LU trains more chaplains than any other institution, with over nine hundred chaplain candidates in current enrollment. The school's online Military Affairs Office is comprised of more than forty military education experts, most of whom are veterans themselves. Active duty military students receive top-notch guidance from leading PTSD experts while accumulating college credits. The stigma of counseling, which prevents so many warriors from receiving help, is removed. This brilliant support program smoothly puts veterans and their families onto a road of recovery and success.

Major General Bob Dees (US Army, Ret.) director of IMR and author of *Resilient Warriors*, states, "In light of the daunting mental and behavioral health trends in our military, we absolutely must get everything in the fight, including help, hope, healing, and resilience through the power of faith. Liberty's IMR is the nation's first faith-based resilience program (relevant curriculum, helpful outreach, evidence-based research) for veterans, troops, and military families; as well as those who provide care and counsel for them."

A major atrocity that *must* be addressed throughout universities nationwide is an "antimilitary" or "anti-veteran" environment. A recent survey revealed that the top challenge veteran students have reported is discomfort in classes where professors appear to be anti-military and where verbal confrontations occur with other students when they share their veteran status. To avoid these confrontations and being labeled and seen only as a veteran, student veterans may hide their veteran status or avoid socializing with their classmates.[18] Liberty University attacks this abomination with fervor by incorporating Military Emphasis Week into its annual schedule. This event raises awareness and appreciation for the military among the students, community, and nation. The weeklong event is filled with patriotic music and veterans' motivational testimonies. Additionally, LU facilitates veteran appreciation by encouraging patriotic students to become involved.

Among the numerous support groups LU offers, one unique student-run organization called Students Behind Our Soldiers (SBS) encourages student/military relationships. This group's vision is to give back to the brave men and women who serve in the US military and their families. This group supports military members through a variety of methods:

- Care packages: collecting donations, packing and shipping packages overseas
- Ministering to patients in veteran hospitals
- Ministering to family members of those serving in the military
- Various outreach efforts on campus and in the local community

In addition to increasing student awareness, General Dees assists faculty orientation with seminars such as "Educating and Empowering Military Students." These seminars are designed to ensure that resident and online faculty understand the military culture and

18. Chris Andrew Cate, Michael Gerber, and David L Holmes, "A New Generation of Student Veterans: A Pilot Study," 11 November 2010.

unique challenges soldiers face on the battlefront, on the home front, and in the classroom.

In 2012 LU's military enrollment soared to 25,000 (300 residents). Seven hundred military students attended a military graduation where each military graduate (including those deployed or unable to attend) is recognized for his or her service and receives a military coin and the affirmation of distinguished military leaders in attendance.

If you are a combat veteran and are deciding where to attend college, look for one that not only provides excellent military support, but one that also has proven military success. If your school does not offer veteran support programs, present these programs to your student affairs or veterans' office. Visit LU's and UCM's veterans' websites for more information. Consider enrolling in IMR's online courses.

I ran into Joe weeks after our initial meeting. I asked him how college life was treating him. He said, "I found a place where I feel I belong—the student vet center. I'm meeting other veterans like me. I don't know if I'd stay here [college] without it."

Dear Lord, help our warriors transition from combat/military life into civilian and college life. Place a fiery passion in the hearts of leadership and students to reach out and help our veterans who sacrifice all so we may exercise the freedoms that we hold dear.

IF YOU ARE A MILITARY VETERAN, what resources are you using to help reintegrate from combat to civilian life? Check out the Institute of Military Resiliency for their online or campus courses.

Do you have a heart to help our military but don't know where to begin? Visit your student Veteran's Affair Center or Student Affairs office and volunteer. Suggest some of the mentioned programs. Are you college shopping? Research schools with a supportive veteran's center and connect with fellow student veterans.

Resources

See appendix B, "Combat-Related Stress Helps." An especially helpful resource that is a *must* for every veteran transitioning back into civilian and campus life is *Once a Warrior: Wired for Life* by Bridget C. Cantrell and Chuck Dean and the accompanying *Once a Warrior: Wired for Life* workbook.

TWENTY-TWO

They Just Don't Think Like Us

Restoring Marital Intimacy

Then Jacob said to Laban, "Give me my wife. My time is completed, and I want to make love to her."

Genesis 29:21

Military aviators have been admiring both beautiful airplanes and women since Orville and Wilbur made the first flight at Kitty Hawk, North Carolina. In fact, when pilots speak of airplanes, they will say, "She's a thing of beauty." The same is true about how males view women. Most men can't help but look when a pretty woman walks by. Looking at a beautiful lady is completely natural, just like blinking when an object gets close to your eye. There's no doubt that God created man with a strong sex drive.

The story of Jacob in Genesis 29 illustrates to what lengths some men will go to satisfy this intrinsic desire. In this Bible passage, Jacob notices Rachel's figure and beauty and offers to work for her father, Laban, for *seven years* to earn her hand in marriage. After completing his agreement, Jacob was tricked to work an additional seven years to marry Rachel. The Scriptures read, "Then Jacob said to Laban, 'Give me my wife. My time is completed, and I want to make love to her.'"

Wow! Imagine that! God created men back in Bible times the same way we are today (Although I think I'd have to renegotiate the deal with the future father-in-law. I don't think I share Jacob's patience!)

We should not be ashamed of our sex drive. God has a plan for meeting our natural needs, and it involves marrying a woman. In the gospel of Matthew, Jesus says, "Haven't you read that at the beginning the Creator 'made them male and female,' and said, 'For this reason a man will leave his father and mother and be united to his wife, and the two will become one flesh?' So they are no longer two, but one flesh. Therefore what God has joined together, let no one separate" (19:4–6). Sex between husband and wife is a wonderful, natural act and an important part of marriage and civilization. Imagine a world that does not have relationships between men and women.

So from this point onward, let's assume that when I bring up the word *sex*, I'm talking about a male married to a woman. In that context, let's explore some findings with the aim of helping men better understand women, while simultaneously achieving sexual satisfaction with your spouse.

The first and most significant finding that will likely shock you is that women, well, they just don't think like us. Case in point: When I asked Penny what I could do to get her in the mood for love, her response floored me. "You can do the dishes, make a nice dinner, or help people in need. That attracts me to you." *What does that have to do with sex?* Penny's interesting response was the catalyst for this research. So here's what I found: Most women's idea of sex is more about romance and intimacy than just the act of sex. Ladies are amazing in that they can multitask. They can talk on the phone and cook dinner while monitoring the kids doing homework. Men can really only do one thing well at a time, and most often can't hold a conversation while doing the task at hand. Most men care about sports, food, and how clean their cars are. On the other hand, most women care about relationships. Get the picture?

Most women wish to be understood. Women are loaded with emotions and feelings, and most are more considerate than men. Women prefer being social and conversational. Women enjoy finding common ground. The only common ground guys understand has to do with sex, food, and sports. All guys need is a good meal, decent shelter, and some good lovemaking, and we're pretty much good to go. Not women. The most significant finding I discovered was that women want to be understood and respected. Once women feel loved and valued, then they're more likely to give love freely. Are you listening, guys? Just ask any lady if this is true to help verify my findings. Men don't need the stars to align in order to have sex, whereas women do. For women, any misunderstanding needs to be resolved to set the mood; children must be settled or asleep; phones must be turned off. In a man's mind, sex resolves arguments; children can tear the house apart outside the bedroom door; the cell phone, the home phone, and Skype can all be screaming simultaneously to be answered, and men won't hear a thing.

Ladies desire in-depth conversation, affection, and nurturing to live a fulfilling life. Their idea of great sex begins with their man planning a dinner or writing a love note that expresses how much he cares for her. Listen up, guys. Women don't fully appreciate the word *sex* and may actually view it as a bit vulgar, but not always. I know this is confusing. Women most often prefer the term *making love* or *intimacy*. I don't have to ask men if they prefer the word *sex*, when they mean sex. Am I right? Women adore flowers and gifts that may have little significance to you, except for the fact that you took time to send them. They'll treasure those love trinkets and place them in a special box. They love romance. So how does a married man gratify his basic need for sex, something he desires as much as oxygen, while simultaneously satisfying his wife's need for love and being valued? Well, it begins with something that's counterintuitive. So here goes, for it's common knowledge that a lack of intimacy can lead to destructive behaviors, such as viewing pornography or having an illicit affair. Let's review some potential solutions to this challenge so we can be better partners.

Military aviators develop tactics, techniques, and procedures (TTPs) to accomplish their operational mission. These TTPs are known as lessons learned passed down by generations of pilots to prevent new pilots from making common mistakes. By writing down TTPs and reviewing them often, pilots are able to fly, fight, and win. Here are some TTPs for you, warrior brothers, to help you engage your resources and make robust plans to help you accomplish your mission of satisfying both parties' desires in a respectful, non-compromising way.

- Make sure to notice when your wife gets her hair done. It's really bad if you don't, and worse still if you say something negative. Remember the saying, "If you don't have something good to say, then don't say it." Repeat this to yourself until you get it.
- Purchase a full-body massage gift certificate for no reason except that you love her and want her relaxed.
- Know special dates that are significant to her and write a hand-written love note on that date.
- Buy her an outfit that she will like—not one that includes a lift-up bra.
- Coordinate child care, dinner reservations, and perhaps a classy hotel room for special occasions, especially your wedding anniversary.
- Bring home fresh-cut flowers.
- Notice her shoes.
- This is a great one, so get ready. Provide her with a totally relaxing weekend away with her girlfriends to give her a break from her chaotic world. This will cause her to reflect on how much she means to you, and it has the added bonus that the ladies will likely talk about "intimacy issues."

The fact that you're really thinking of her and going through all this romantic stuff turns her on . . . I mean, it makes her feel special. Put her needs above your own, and she'll likely want to please you. Your motivation for meeting her needs should be purely out of love and not just for any anticipated reward. When you take time to plan ahead and have a great evening out, don't make it all about your need to have sex. Be authentic and give of your energies and time to make her feel like the apple of your eye—for she should be. When dining out, don't go to a sports bar and face a television monitor. Give her your attention and listen to her. Stay focused and do not be distracted by outsiders. End desired result: the flower will blossom and the aroma of her inner love will cause your eyes to twinkle. Take these TTPs seriously, men.

Now, if you've accomplished these types of TTPs, and you're keeping the communication channels open while being faithful, and she's still not being intimate, then spell it out to her. I mean literally write it down in a letter and explain your feelings. Explain that sex is a biblical thing. Reference 1 Corinthians 7:1–40. While you're at it, make sure she understands that we're not speaking about an annual requirement, but more like a weekly, or maybe even daily need—give or take a day or two. You two will have to figure that out.

Another important TTP that you can do is to shine your armor. If you're out of shape and continually forget to apply deodorant, then it's likely that you're not the most handsome guy out there any longer. Don't walk around with shorts and black socks on! Get rid of that gut and commit to an active lifestyle. Work out daily and keep your body in shape. It will help other aspects of your life as well. Dress up when taking her out on a date, put on some nice cologne before intimate time, and keep smiling. Too many of us are stressed out and take work home. Leave work at the office, and take interest in your wife and family when at home. Look her in the eye when she speaks. Pay attention. Whisper in her ear how beautiful she is, and tell her that you love her. Think about her needs and discover new ways to make her happy, and I assure you that she will respond in a positive way. Did I mention to smile more?

The rewards of properly executing these TTPs are worth the time and effort. Don't ever give up if your spouse refuses to be intimate. There may be underlining causes that you need to investigate, so seek help through counseling. Love is ultimately the answer. "Love is patient, love is kind. It does not envy, it does not boast, it is not proud. It does not dishonor others, it is not self-seeking, it is not easily angered, it keeps no record of wrongs. Love does not delight in evil but rejoices with the truth. It always protects, always trusts, always hopes, always perseveres. Love never fails" (1 Corinthians 13:4–8). Take hope in those words. Try to understand her needs and don't make it all about yours. Give her space and help her deal with her feelings or other issues preventing her from being close to you. Don't seek satisfaction elsewhere from other ladies or pornography, for that will only lead to personal destruction. Pray for God's intervention and power.

When Penny and I went through serious marriage problems, I dealt with these issues firsthand. If you're experiencing a lack of intimacy with your spouse, I encourage you to stay true to your marriage. God's Word is clear that we're not to commit adultery. Never give up in your quest to satisfy each other's needs. Keep trying to make things better in your relationship and be part of the solution and not the problem. Be a man of character and be true to yourself, God, and your spouse. It's my sincere hope that you have found this information informative and enlightening. Now go execute these TTPs and enjoy "intimacy" with your wife.

God, you made us the way we are. Give us wisdom when dealing with our sexual needs. Help us find common ground with our spouses. Help me place my spouse's needs over my own.

ARE YOU HAVING INTIMACY CHALLENGES with your wife? How are you putting your spouse's needs over yours? When was the last time you surprised her with an unexpected gift? Are you willing to rely on love to get you through the tough times?

Resources
- *The Five Love Languages* by Gary Chapman
- *Sheet Music: Uncovering the Secrets of Sexual Intimacy in Marriage* by Dr. Kevin Leman
- *Sex Begins in the Kitchen* by Dr. Kevin Leman
- *His Needs, Her Needs: Building an Affair-Proof Marriage* by Willard F. Harley Jr.
- *We All Married Idiots: Three Things You Will Never Change About Your Marriage and Ten Things You Can* by Elaine W. Miller

See appendix C for book descriptions.

TWENTY-THREE

Stay in the Boat

Trusting God During Life's Storms

*When you pass through the waters, I will be with you.
When you pass through the rivers, they will not flow over
you. . . . For I am the Lord your God, the Holy One of
Israel, Who saves you.*

*Isaiah 43:2–3,
New Life Version*

I scanned the enormous room filled with army spouses from Fort
Riley, Kansas. "One?" I asked. Nearly every hand in the room was
raised "Two?" About the same amount of hands shot up. I upped
the ante. "Three?" Over half the room's hands rose into the air. I
kept increasing the number and finally stopped as the last hand raised
when I asked, "Seven?" putting an end to my question: "How many
deployments lasting six to twelve months have you experienced in
the last ten years?" *Okay*, I prayed. *God, do your stuff!*

Months of diligent prayer, during which I asked God to deliver His strength to the brave, hurting army spouses of Fort Riley, preceded this presentation. Two battalions that suffered tremendous casualties and sustained severely wounded soldiers due to combat in Iraq and Afghanistan were soon returning. Anxiety plagued many home-front spouses who did not know what to expect when their warriors transitioned back into "normal" life. The home-front spouses needed tools to weather potential storms, ones that may brew in their own homes.

In addition to normal life pressures, the added stressors of military life, including multiple deployments and impaired communication, may rage like a turbulent sea, and to many military couples, divorce masquerades itself as a life preserver to prevent drowning; however, a much better lifeline exists.

"Stay in the boat!" I encouraged. "God often allows life's storms for reasons we don't understand. After Jesus' disciples obediently doled out fish and bread to approximately five thousand people, which actually totaled over ten thousand because women and children were not counted, Jesus summoned the energy-drained disciples to hop into a boat and paddle the long journey to Bethsaida (Mark 6:45–51). After catering to a crowd the size of a small city, I'm afraid that my response might be more like, "Really, Jesus? We just fed thousands of travelers, and now you want us to row across the Sea of Galilee? In the dark? With not even a flashlight to guide us? Sorry, but my servant's energy left with the last table of thirteen from Judea."

Thankfully, the disciples responded differently. The burned-out bunch boarded the boat and complied with Jesus' request while He stayed behind. Then aggressive winds rolled in, tossing the disciples' boat like a leaf in a storm while Jesus watched from a mountainside. Why didn't Jesus snap His fingers and calm the gales when He saw His faithful friends challenged by the wind's force? Picturing Jesus just watching while the apostles fought to stay afloat used to frustrate me. Jesus let them row and row into the storm from sunset until the fourth watch, around three a.m. By letting His exhausted friends suffer through the raging waves without intervening, Jesus taught the disciples one of the greatest lessons they would ever learn, one that would toughen them for all storms yet to come. They learned how to recognize Jesus in the storm.

When Jesus finally steps out onto the water, at first the disciples think He is a ghost, and the storm lingers on. As He approaches the boat, they recognize that the form is no apparition; it's Jesus, and the storm immediately subsides. Had the disciples jumped ship during the raging storm, they could have drowned.

Often we don't recognize Jesus in the midst of our suffering. We become self-absorbed. If we throw in the marriage towel or take the next drink before trusting God, we will never reap the blessings conceived from the storm. Although we may think God is deaf to our rescue cries as we row through a marital storm, a child's rebellious behavior, financial instability, or an addictive behavior, God knows exactly where we are, and He clearly sees our challenges. He hears our heart's cry.

Once, while struggling through our Category 5 marital storm, I remember closing the car windows in an empty parking lot, pounding on the steering wheel, and yelling at God (yes, yelling), "Why don't you answer me? I'm asking you to piece my broken marriage together! Isn't that what you want too?" My husband and I battled daily. The relentless stress exhausted me and was adversely affecting my physical health as well. At one point I wanted to bail out; I asked for a legal separation so I could spare my children and me from continuously walking on eggshells for fear of angry outbursts. Thankfully, Tony objected to the separation and refused to leave the boat, but at the time, I felt more lost than ever. We didn't like each other. In fact, during those times, we felt hatred toward each other. Regardless, we decided to honor our marriage vows and remain in the boat together while the sea continued to rage around us.

Looking back, I'm grateful that the Lord did not immediately run down the mountainside and rescue that pitiful woman crying in the parking lot. If He had, the storms would not have exposed our relationship's impurities, which were stunting our marriage's growth. Our relationship would not have been refined into the beautiful union it is today. Little did I know that while I felt abandoned in the storm, not only was God gutting the sinful decay within my own built-up walls, but His heavenly wrecking ball was also tearing down Tony's sinful defects. Through an extreme marital makeover, the storm washed away the walls and transformed our relationship into a beautiful creation—for His purpose.

Every married couple periodically finds themselves rowing through life's storms and questioning their strength to make the journey. Sometimes, storms build gradually. Other times, our lives leap overnight from calmness into a tumultuous hurricane. We find ourselves hard-pressed to make tough decisions. Well-meaning friends may advise us to jump ship, which normally isn't God's direction.[19] Do we leave our spouse and search for greener pastures? Do we take another drink or pop another pill to numb our pain? Do we slander our spouse's character through gossip? Do we reject God because of unmet dreams or broken promises? We can remain obedient to God's commands and trust Him fully, or we can choose what appears to be the easy way out by looking to worldly answers, which in the end cause destruction to ourselves and our relationship with God, while raining collateral damage onto our children and generations to come.

You may be in the midst of a storm right now and are blind to what lies ahead. Maybe you have located a looming funnel cloud and are dreading its imminent touchdown. Commit to honor your marriage vows *before* the storm sets in. We all sin, and we must forgive routine trivial matters such as not loading the dishwasher so we can handle much more serious afflictions. Love covers a multitude of sins. Tony and I both believed that we had to possess supernatural strength to forgive, but our weak selves were incapable of doing this alone. Only through Christ's redemptive love flowing through us are we empowered to truly forgive.

Walking by faith includes obeying God when we do not understand why we are suffering. Submit to honor the "for worse" part of

---

19. Never remain in a situation where you are fearful for your or your children's safety. If you have to leave, reassure your spouse that leaving a dangerous situation is not equivalent to giving up on your marriage. Seek safety immediately. If your spouse refuses to go to marriage counseling with you, go by yourself. Your spouse is likely to follow if he sees the positive impact counseling has on you. Get help from your installation's victim advocate—the Family Support Center or Family Advocacy Program will connect you. Or call Military OneSource at 1-800-342-9647, or the National Domestic Violence Hotline at 1-800-799-SAFE.

the marriage vows without understanding the "whys" when storms approach. Understanding often comes *after* obedience, not before. Pray and seek counsel to calm the roughest waves. Prayer and godly counsel were the lifelines that kept our marriage from drowning and helped us discover that solutions to our challenges lay within us—not in jumping ship. Don't let pride stand in the way of God's rescue line. Recognize *who* is with you in the storm instead of focusing on the bad weather. Accept Jesus' outstretched hand. He will never let you go.

Dear heavenly Father, thank You for calling me by name and caring for me during the storms. Help me to recognize Your strengthening presence and to obey Your commands when I feel like jumping ship. Thank You for promising to never let me go.

HAVE YOU COMMITTED to stay in the boat when the waters get rough? What threatening fronts can you see moving in? A deployment, homecoming, relocation, retirement? What proactive measures can you take now to strengthen your relationship?

Resources

Focus on the Family will help you to find a Christian marriage counselor in your area. See appendix C for the web address and instructions. To weatherproof your marriage from future storms, take the "Communication Tune-up for Couples" in appendix A.

PART 5

Transition into the
Civilian World

TWENTY-FOUR

Bagel Opportunities

Making Your Dream a Reality

Be wise in the way you act toward outsiders; make the most of every opportunity.

Colossians 4:5,
NIV (1984)

I vividly recall when my dad bought my mother our first washer and dryer. Prior to having a washing machine, Mom washed our clothes in the sink and hung them on clotheslines in the alleyway of our Brooklyn home. The clothes would be in the way as we played baseball. My dad asked where she wanted the washing machine, and she pointed at a wall in the basement. I asked how my dad planned on connecting the water and electric lines to the new appliances. What was the plan? I began measuring the area and asked for any architectural documents that we could reference.

My dad responded with a grin on his face, saying, "Son. Let me show you how we'll do it. Could you please pass me that hammer?"

He then proceeded to slam the hammer into the wall at the exact location my mom wanted the appliances. He placed his hands into the now-busted sheetrock and made a bigger hole while stating, "Sometimes you just have to act." I couldn't believe it. In a matter of minutes, he figured everything out, and after a few more holes, he made it happen. Right before my eyes, I witnessed a man of action. He later explained that we would need to re-sheetrock and paint anyway, so why waste so much time planning? His message was clear: "If the solution is clear and can be done now, then err toward doing it."

Another person who influenced me is my brother Giuliano. He knows only one speed: GO! He's always going forward like a tank on a mission. Toward the end of my initial Air Force career, after returning from an overseas assignment, my family and I traveled to Giuliano's house in Indianapolis to retrieve my sports car. The day before my family and I planned to return to base, he asked if I wanted to join him to buy some fresh bagels. On the way to the bagel store, he showed me the restaurant he and his partners created.

When I walked into this quaint, open-kitchen style Italian restaurant, an idea flashed in my mind. My new assignment was at Whiteman Air Force Base, Missouri, and I knew there was no authentic Italian food within thirty miles of the base. I asked Giuliano, "Why not start a restaurant with me?" He loved the idea! With his Brooklyn accent, while waving his hands as if orchestrating music, he said, "Bro, if you invest the money and help me with strategy and training, I can run the restaurant, and then fogetaboutit. Listen, Bro," he continued, "here's what's gonna happen: as one hand washes the other, together we'll wash the face!" And that's when I started laughing at my little brother's enthusiasm and spirit. On that day, a "bagel opportunity" popped up, and the genesis of Monetti's Pizzeria Ristorante was born.

Within three months, we had created a business plan, secured financing, and bought and transformed a video store into our family restaurant. In 2011, we were voted one of the Top 10 unique eateries in the state of Missouri. In 2012, my brother opened a new restaurant near Kansas City called Monetti's—A Taste of Italy. The education and lessons learned over the years equates to a PhD in how to run a restaurant. But that's another book for another day loaded with lots of drama and excitement. My father's "make it happen now attitude" influenced my brother and me to take on new challenges with determination and quick action. The opportunity presented itself, and we ran with it.

If you're getting ready to hang up the military uniform in search of a civilian job, you have a major leg up on those who have not served. You have served alongside heroes, and you have been responsible for demanding missions under some of the most severe situations. You've flown supersonic, shot at enemy forces, maneuvered a satellite, or commanded a ship on the high seas. You've been part of international teams and are highly trained and educated. Your past experiences will define you. Your service to America makes you strong today and marketable in the future. Your skills in leading small teams to accomplish missions make you an ideal candidate for future challenges. As you transition, have confidence in yourself and go after the job you want. Resist the temptation to go after the sure thing as you transition to new jobs. Trying to figure out what you will do for the next part of your life sure isn't easy, so give it time. Seek counsel from people you respect.

Here is one way to think about getting advice: Make a fist and allow it to remind you to seek the counsel of five good people. Think of the thumb as your main person you value and trust most, such as your parent or spouse. Choose four other people that have your best interest in mind and listen to their combined wisdom. These mentors should be people who rejoice in your past accomplishments and love you. If they are all pointing like fingers in the same direction, then I suggest you take their mentoring advice, and remember that you're never alone. Pray to God and rely on His eternal perspective. A sage army veteran and experienced counselor, Colonel Phil Pringle, shared that veterans in transition should "Be still and listen to the right voice." I think his advice is spot-on. By seeking the counsel of friends and going to God for direction, you can make the best decision possible.

As I was coming up on retirement my second time around after accepting a voluntary recall to active duty, I planned on using my flying skills to work for an airline. A voice inside me yearned to use the leadership skills acquired from my military career. I enjoyed mentoring youth, but my practical skills were centered on flying, and the airlines were hiring. An airline position would provide security for my family, but the small voice still echoed doubt. I prayed with my wife for God to open and close the doors for my next career and lead me to a job He knew would be best for my family and me. My good friends and acquaintances helped me get an opportunity for an interview with FedEx Airlines—a pilot's dream job; however, after months of preparation, a new opportunity presented itself.

The University of Central Missouri, located in the same town as our home, was looking for a change of direction for its aviation program. The best way to explain how I was hired in the newly created position of assistant dean of aviation and executive director of Skyhaven Airport was to say that it was beyond serendipity. Everything, and I mean everything, seemed to fall in place. I accepted the new position, which afforded me the opportunity to do what I love most: flying and encouraging young people to live their dreams. Each day I go to work, I'm excited about my job because I am able to use my skills to help others succeed.

"Bagel opportunities" exist all over. The question is, are you ready for a new adventure? As you transition, do you know what you would like to do with your life? Are you working toward specific goals and ambitions, or are you just settling? As you prepare for new adventures, I encourage you to go for it and live your dreams while praying for God's direction. I've heard it said that nothing succeeds like success. Being successful is rewarding, but success is not something issued while you're standing in line. You have to go for it. You have to act! You have to earn it. Through my experiences, I've learned that *the key to success is helping others succeed.* The men and women who influenced my life were instrumental in bringing me one step closer to achieving my life's goals. In turn, I've gained satisfaction by helping others succeed, and it goes on. I encourage you to go create your own successful life story. Live a life of little regret, for there's no better place in the world to achieve your dreams than in America. Life is too short to say, "I wish I would have . . ." so why not grab the hammer and act? Go for it now.

Heavenly Father, open the doors You want for me to walk through and close those that lead me away from Your will. Afford me the courage to chart a new course and place wise people along the way to mentor and guide me.

WHAT "BAGEL OPPORTUNITIES" do you see on your horizon? How can you incorporate your talents into your ambitions? Are you helping others succeed along the way?

Resources

Are you wondering what to do after the military? Plan now! Assess your skills, interests, values, personality, and leisure time preferences to piece together a career choice that will be the right fit for you. Visit www.ucmo.edu/gateway. Click on the "Focus" tab on the left tool bar. Start a free account within minutes, and get ready! Numerous assessments will link you to compatible career choices where you can explore salaries, skill and education requirements, and much more.

Also check out O Net Online (onetonline.org), which lets you see how your military skills transfer into civilian careers. Once at the site, click "Crosswalks," and then "Military." This resource transfers military skills into compatible civilian careers based on your military occupation specialty (MOS). This resource is an absolute treasure for military warriors transitioning into the civilian realm.

TWENTY-FIVE

Your Dad Goes Before You

Keeping Communication Lines Open

*"The Lord himself goes before you and will be with you;
he will never leave you nor forsake you. Do not be afraid;
do not be discouraged."*

Deuteronomy 31:8

"It hurts you more, Dad, because you pampered fly boys just can't
hack the pain," Antonio announced.

Tony jokingly counterattacked with: "No! Your doctor knew a
sniveling army grunt couldn't withstand a complex procedure like
mine and made your surgery a picnic."

Playful bantering over which service was tougher became common dinner conversation once our son, Antonio, enlisted into the
Army Reserves while in ROTC[20] at the local university. Tony had
recently undergone the same sinus surgery that Antonio endured
years earlier. The two rams continued butting heads in the *who is*

---

20. Reserve Officers' Training Corps.

tougher game until Tony switched gears midway, "Well, the B-2s are the first planes to storm into enemy territory and pave the way for you ground-pounders. We remove the threats before you advance into the danger zone."

Tony's comment created a mental picture I couldn't ignore. "Wow, how cool would that be, Antonio, if your *own* dad flew the B-2 to clear the enemy threats before your platoon marched in? How awesome would it be telling your buddies, 'Hey that's my dad flying up there. We're safe cause he's looking out for us.'" My question sparked thought, and for the first time during our dinner, a pensive lull replaced the verbal sparring match.

Then it hit me. The idea of Tony flying overhead before his son entered unknown territory illustrated one of my favorite Bible verses, which has strengthened me numerous times during the past twenty-five years of military life and continues to encourage me now that my son is enlisted: "The Lord himself goes before you and will be with you; he will never leave you nor forsake you. Do not be afraid; do not be discouraged" (Deuteronomy 31:8).

Just as the military's air power clears a path for ground troops to safely complete their missions, our Father in heaven goes before us in all of life's transitions and challenges. Whether our unknown territory exists on the home front, overseas, or within our own thoughts, God goes before us. He provides coordinates to stay on course, but it is our responsibility to keep the direct line of communication open so we don't lose our way.

A military pilot removes threats for the troops below, but direct communication is key to a successful mission. Tony conveyed an incident regarding a B-1 bomber pilot who received a request for immediate air support from an army lieutenant as his men were under attack by overwhelming enemy forces in Afghanistan. The B-1 crew placed precision weapons on target, saving many American soldiers. The lieutenant's accurate information helped the B-1 crew accomplish their mission. Just as relaying vital information between the air and ground units is crucial for a successful, safe mission, so is consistent communication with God the key to living an abundant, joy-filled life, regardless of the struggles we encounter. In combat, if communication lines are disabled, the mission may falter and lives can be jeopardized. If we don't keep our communication channels flowing between us and God, we can dangerously veer off course into unhealthy behaviors and injure ourselves and those we love.

An expert in B-2 technology (a man I happen to live with) explained that pilots communicate with ground forces through a "nine line." Nine numbers with several subcategory buttons ensure that crucial information is accurately transmitted between the pilot and ground forces with minimal radio correspondence for safety precautions. When specific numbers are entered, the pilot and ground unit share pertinent information, such as a target's description, if a friendly location is nearby, and the command to abort a mission. This communication link is a lifeline to the ground forces, connecting them to air power.

You have your own personal "nine line" that connects you directly to your air power—God. Your special connection to our Father above is already in place, or you would not be holding this book in your hands right now. Scripture contains all the "nine line" buttons needed to guide us to a victorious life. Using this direct "nine line" to God helps us gain wisdom to victoriously overcome challenges and threats. This spiritual connection eliminates life's static that interferes with our peace and joy, such as fear, worry, anxiety, anger, loneliness, bitterness, and temptations.

Just as military air power paves the way for the ground troops by clearing threats beforehand, God goes before you in your life transitions and daily challenges. The military's "nine line" effectively unites the Army, Air Force, Marines, Navy, Coast Guard, and Reserves to achieve missions and avoid dangerous threats. Our spiritual "nine lines" unite us with the ultimate power source—God.

By using our "nine lines" daily, we can eliminate threats so we can be effective warriors in His army and live an abundant life. If we do stray off course from time to time, our "nine lines" will assure we find our way back. Do you utilize your "nine line" daily? If not, there's no better day to begin than today.

Dear heavenly Father, thank You for going out before me daily and providing a direct link of communication through prayer and Your Holy Word to keep me focused on Your direction for my life. Give me the desire and opportunities to access my "nine line" daily.

HOW DO YOU UTILIZE your "nine line" to God? Do you stay in communication with God when life becomes busy? How may this communication process change in life's different seasons? Give some examples of how reading Scripture affects your daily life. What other "nine line" examples connect you with God?

Resources

Numerous websites offer daily Scripture that can be sent to your e-mail or phone, and daily devotionals like *Our Daily Bread* keep our "nine lines" open for communication. Military chaplains can provide a Bible if you do not own one. For devotional recommendations and other Bible study resources, see appendix C.

TWENTY-SIX

Bag of Cement

Achieving Success

*Hope deferred makes the heart sick, but a longing fulfilled
is a tree of life.*

Proverbs 13:12

Prior to flying jets for the greatest air force in the world, I had the privilege of being mentored by a self-made millionaire. In 1956 Gennaro Sbarro emigrated from Naples, Italy, to the USA in search of the American dream, and he found it. I worked for Mr. Sbarro at his first *salumeria* (grocery store) during my high school years in Brooklyn, New York. Sbarro's Italian Salumeria was known for its authentic, fresh, homemade Italian cuisine. Mr. Sbarro shared a vision with me that "Sbarro's" would someday be all over America and the world. Besides catering for large parties, we sold Italian style subs and homemade pizza.

Mr. Sbarro was a short man in stature but huge in life. He was the hardest working person I've ever known. Mr. Sbarro was instrumental in forming the person I am today, and besides my mom and dad, his life shaped my way of thinking more than anyone else. When I first met him while searching for after-school work, he offered me a job on the spot. We spoke about family and my dream to fly jets for the US Air Force. I explained my passion for flying and why I attended Aviation High School, which required three hours of daily commute.

During our initial encounter, we spoke in our first language, Italian. I was born in America after my parents immigrated here, whereas Mr. Sbarro earned his citizenship on his own. On my first day at work, he gave me an envelope filled with hundreds of dollars from the previous night's earnings and asked me to deposit the money at a local bank. Amazingly, he trusted me with the monies, even though he didn't know my full name or address. Without hesitation, every cent was deposited, and thus began my journey with the Sbarro family. It was a relationship based on trust and mutual respect.

One evening, while getting ready to close, Mr. Sbarro noticed I was mopping. He said, "That's not how you do it. Here, give me the mop." He proceeded to scrub hard, putting lots of effort into it, until the entire floor was clean. The brow of his forehead formed beads of sweat that fell on the floor. He wasn't putting on a show. He was giving it his all to impress upon me the need to do things right. When you're mopping, mop hard, and get it done right. He encouraged me to give everything my best effort—and not just with mopping. He taught me to give a 100 percent, especially when no one was looking. The mopping lesson was followed later by the "bag of cement story," which marked a turning point in my life.

One day, Mr. Sbarro asked me to buy a bag of cement to fix a loose pipe in the store's restroom. After I returned with the purchase, he asked me to fix it. "I don't know how to cement, Mr. Sbarro," I replied. He winced his left eye, pointed at me, and said in his Italian accent, "Whatta you meana, you don't knowa how to cementa? You know how to read? Then read the instructions and do it. Remember Raffaele, you canna do anything you putta your mind to!" Part of me was offended at his stern tone, but I decided to take him up on his challenge and proceeded to read the instructions.

Thus began my life lesson, one sentence at a time—on the back of a cement bag. He stood behind me the entire time, rocking on his heels with his arms crossed while adding, "You can and willa do this, and if you have problems, I'ma here for you." When I mixed the powder with water, cement began forming and I soon fixed the loose pipe. Before my eyes, it transformed into a usable substance, and I understood his message. I smiled at him with a deep sense of accomplishment and satisfaction that I could do this and so much more. Mr. Sbarro stood behind me, still bobbing up and down while posting a huge smile on his face. I understood his strong message that *you can* do anything you put your mind to. He was right then, and his lesson lives on today.

Mr. Sbarro was disappointed years later when I decided to leave his family business to pursue my dreams of flying jets for the Air Force, but he understood that I had to do what I had to do. My dream was realized when I was accepted into the Air Force Academy, which provided the gateway to my wings so I could fly jets.

Mr. Sbarro's vision became a reality of over a thousand restaurants in more than forty countries. Not a bad food empire for an Italian immigrant who learned English in the streets of Brooklyn. Each year, when returning home on leave, I would stop by and chat with the Sbarro family. After Mr. Sbarro passed away, his wife Carmella returned to the very first Sbarro's store behind the counter where the dream began. She was an amazing lady and served as the wind behind his sails. It was truly a privilege knowing the Sbarro family.

His legacy of teaching me the importance of hard work, coupled with perseverance, helped form me into the man I am today. His lesson holds true for anyone who understands the importance of showing up, living your dreams, and seeking new opportunities. Knowing that you can do anything you put your mind to is essential in life. Having that unshakable belief in yourself is essential to success. Living in America, the land of opportunity, is a great blessing. America encourages innovation and free enterprise. All you need is an idea, fueled with passion, ability, and determination to fulfill your dream. As you transition from the military to the civilian world, and yes it is a completely different world, allow me to encourage you to dream big.

As a teenager looking for an after-school job, I knocked on many doors before Mr. Sbarro answered and gave me a shot. Although I didn't follow his desire to build Sbarro restaurants, he taught me valuable life lessons that I've treasured. His wisdom and example helped me achieve my dreams and aspirations. In turn, I gained the confidence to "go for it," and within years after Sbarro's, I was flying supersonic jets. I know the thrill of pulling nine Gs and then pointing a jet straight up into the sky while accelerating upward and onward while strapped in a MIG 29 in Hungary. I've flown over all of the world's oceans and soared over the highest mountains just five hundred feet above rugged terrain traveling at seven hundred knots. Flying supersonic never gets old! I witnessed meteor showers brightening the desert night sky while air refueling behind a KC10 tanker in a B-1 variable swept wing bomber. I've seen the skies light up as if hundreds of fireworks displays were going off simultaneously during the initial strikes against heavily fortified enemy forces. Flying the most expensive aircraft ever built—worth more than its weight in gold, the B-2 Spirit—was completely awe-inspiring. In addition, I was privileged to serve with some amazing fellow airmen.

That chance encounter with a small-statured man and his bag-of-cement lesson provided me with a strong sense of determination. It also showed me that you can live your dreams and live a fulfilling life. When you work hard and give something all you've got and succeed in your ambitions, well, it just doesn't get much better than that. If he didn't push me out of my comfort zone to make things happen, then who knows where I'd be? Thank you, Mr. Sbarro. The cement is formed and others are learning from you still.

Heavenly Father, help me to see new perspectives. Thank You for allowing me to live in a free country where all things are possible. Surround me with positive people to lift me up and give me the strength to live my dreams.

HOW ARE YOU LIVING your life fully? What ambitions would you like to achieve? Are you happy with your life choices? If not, what are those dreams?

TWENTY-SEVEN

What's Your Jungatee?

Taking Care of Yourself

A cheerful heart is good medicine, but a crushed spirit dries up the bones.

Proverbs 17:22

It was spectacular! The quaint alpine ski school was nestled into the base of the Zugspitze Alp, the tallest mountain in Germany. My kids would soon be skiing on the same slopes as the 1936 winter Olympians. I calmed my eager clan long enough to fit them with skis and boots, filled out the necessary paperwork stating that we wouldn't sue in case of broken bones or other injuries, and then dropped them off in their respective ski classes. I ignored the other skiers' puzzled looks as I toted a computer case instead of ski poles, and hiked instead of skied to the outdoor cafe located at the first ski run's base. Because of previous knee injuries, I was unable to ski with my kids, so I created an outdoor workspace on a picnic table and prepared for a long afternoon of writing and watching my children ski in the amazing winter postcard setting.

The sun reflected each snowflake, creating a crystal-like path that invited skiers of all ages and nationalities to weave and swoosh down this effervescent course. The savory aromas of fresh pine and grilling *sauerbraten* floated in and out with the gentle breeze, magnifying the sensory extravaganza. I watched my little dots quickly enlarge into excited children as they skied within earshot, yelling, "Hey, Mom, did you see me?" Unable to slow down for my reply, they would whoosh off to board the next gondola, transporting them back to the mountaintop to repeat the process. As I soaked in the magnificent scenery and heard the "shoooshes" of skiers, the cafe's outdoor speakers blasted the most cheerful music my ears ever heard. I couldn't understand one German lyric, but the music's upbeat melody was so lively and fun that I didn't care. The exhilarating songs captured my elated mood.

The cheery music, picturesque scenery, warm sunshine, and fun-filled week prompted me to ask the cafe worker in my "Guten tag" limited vocabulary about the music. After several attempts at communicating, I saw understanding finally dawn on the gray-haired cashier. She retrieved a plastic CD case entitled *Jungatee*. I gathered my snow-encrusted, skied-out kids, and returned the ski equipment. We set off to explore the snow-globe-looking German village in search of a music store. After finding the music, we played *Jungatee* wherever we drove. The contagious, perky music infected my kids, and soon we were all singing lyrics that we couldn't understand—together.

Till this day, whenever I need a pick-me-up, I play the *Jungatee* music. Immediately, I slip from the day's stress and time-travel back to that beautiful day on the Bavarian mountainside where I watched my happy kids enjoy a new experience while we savored the sweet music and smells of a new, exciting culture. These uplifting songs magically melt away stress and cheer my heart.

We all need to find our *Jungatee* songs in life. As you grow your families, pursue careers, or approach retirement, it is easy to get so weighed down with life's demands that you put self-care and personal goals on the shelf. Deployments, family health challenges, and normal daily stress can overwhelm you if you're not proactive. Family and friends lean on your strength, and in order to be that fortress of strength during military challenges, you must take care of yourself. You must find *your* "Jungatee." What "Jungatee" removes stress from your busy life? Carve away at least one hour each day from your busy schedule to reenergize your batteries with personal time. Whether you swing at golf balls, plant flowers, or train for a marathon, when you care for yourself by incorporating "Jungatee" time, life flows smoother and you become a better you—for yourself—and those you love.

By praying for God's direction and setting daily, monthly, yearly, five-year, and even ten-year goals, you will discover long-lasting satisfaction. Balancing daily life and personal goals is challenging, but a refreshed and happier self will have a ripple effect into all areas of your life. Ask for family support. Invite the entire family to set goals together so you can support each other's "Jungatee" time, personal goals, and yes, your dreams.

Even when our children were young, we would schedule a time to set annual goals. We encourage spiritual growth and altruism as part of their goals as well. At first, my children dreaded sitting around a table to talk about the next year's plans. Their future focused on the next hour and finding an available friend to go skateboarding, not the upcoming year. As each year passed, however, they realized the value of setting personal and family goals. Our children now glean satisfaction when reviewing their past year's accomplishments at our annual meeting. Tony reviews our progress after six months and helps us to achieve our goals. Our meetings have transformed from numbered lists on scratch paper to sophisticated PowerPoint presentations, seasoned with movie clips and music. Last year, my free-spirited daughter acted her goals out in an entertaining, hilarious presentation. It's amazing to witness your children's sense of accomplishment as they fulfill what they actually set out to achieve.

By setting family goals, you become aware of each other's ambitions, are in tune with each other's dreams, and can help each other to achieve them. Designate a family day to discuss each other's short- and long-term goals. Let family members know in advance so they can prepare. Encourage, never minimize, each other's interests and goals. God created unique passions in each of us, and it's important to embrace those differences.

The years will sneak up and steal your dreams if you don't proactively pursue them now. In an eye's blink, you will wave your child off to pursue his or her own dreams, sign military out-processing papers, and likely hold a beloved grandchild in your arms. Make "Jungatee" time now to renew your health, mind, and spirit. Set goals to achieve your individual and family's dreams, and when you accidentally happen upon new "Jungatee" music that's unplanned, have fun and take advantage of new opportunities. Then, when you are receiving the senior citizen discount at the neighborhood buffet and wonder, "Where did the time go?" you will reflect on fulfilled ambitions with no regrets of what you wish you would have done.

Dear Lord, sometimes I feel selfish taking "me time." Help me rejuvenate, rest, and enjoy the passions You created within me so I can be the best parent, friend, and spouse to those You place in my life. Help me direct my personal and family goals now to create a rich and fulfilling future for myself and those I love.

LIST THREE ACTIVITIES OR HOBBIES that make you cheerful just thinking about them. Schedule "Jungatee" time into your daily routine. Do you feel too busy for goal planning or "Jungatee" time? If you don't create that needed respite, the result might be stress, illness, and a crushed spirit. Would you think differently about taking "me time" if you realized that whatever action you use to manage stress and achieve goals today will likely be your children's same strategy tomorrow?

Resources
- **The Military Spouse Career Advancement Accounts** (www.aiportal.acc.af.mil/mycaa/) provides up to four thousand dollars of financial assistance to eligible military spouses who

are pursuing a license, certification, or Associate's degree in a portable career field and occupation.

- **Military One Source** (www.militaryonesource.mil) provides numerous career resources. Go to the website, click "Spouse Education," and then "Career Opportunities."

TWENTY-EIGHT

Finish Strong

Ending Your Military Career Well

I have fought the good fight, I have finished the race, I have kept the faith.

2 Timothy 4:7

"Wanna fly my 'fini-flight' with me?" asked Lt. Col. Kevin "Psych" Ward. Psych was retiring, and having a fini-flight is one of the most treasured traditions of the Air Force. The day began with checking the weather, conducting a formation flight briefing, and then stepping to the jet for a 09:00 takeoff. It was a cold, crisp day at Whiteman Air Force Base, Missouri, as we strapped into our T-38 Talon rocket. It was a bit more challenging with the extra weight—of the cold weather gear, not the twenty-five pounds we had both gained since our first flight many moons ago. As Psych reviewed the before-starting-engine checklist, he cocked his head to the side and looked over at the mighty B-2 stealth bomber parked nearby on the flight line as the sun rose over the hangars. He just sat there for a minute before pushing the start button. I was synched with Psych and took it all in. Nothing needed to be said, as I understood what he was thinking while reflecting over our twenty-plus year career.

We taxied onto the runway with another T-38 alongside ours. After smoothly advancing the throttles and selecting maximum afterburners, our T-38 Talon aircraft shot forward like a champagne cork set free. We were at 160 knots in seconds as we raised the gear and flaps for the last time and pointed the nose upward toward the blue skies. We danced with the clouds as the other T-38 flew off of our wing a few feet away. After checking our "G" suit, we climbed to 15,000 feet at 500 knots and pulled the jet to five Gs to perform our acclimation maneuvers. These maneuvers prepared our bodies for acrobatics and confirmed that the G-suits were working properly (to prevent us from passing out) before executing over-the-top maneuvers. Psych lowered the nose of our T-38 toward the ground and attained 500 knots while confirming that we had plenty of airspace above us to perform acrobatic maneuvers. He pulled back on the stick for a loop and then performed a few barrel rolls.

After twenty minutes of acrobatics, we exchanged leads, and now we were wingmen. After cranking and banking for another twenty minutes, we returned to the pattern and performed multiple overhead patterns as we practiced touch-and-go landings. Watching the ground whiz by as he rolled the jet on its side and sliced through the horizon was exhilarating. The same excitement that we shared over twenty years earlier when we were first blessed to fly for the Air

Force remained within us. The tower sent us around for one last pass as Psych lit the afterburners.

After landing, we attended a luncheon crammed with aviators young and old to pay their respects to this great instructor pilot and warrior. I sat by Psych and listened as he shared some war stories and nuggets of wisdom. After the commander gave him a farewell gift and touching speech, Psych turned to say a few words. He praised his friends and explained how much it meant for him to be surrounded by so many great patriots.

We made our way back to the squadron for a traditional "naming ceremony" for recent B-2 pilot graduates. The ceremony is an aviator gathering where older pilots decide on nicknames for new members of the flying squadron. Years earlier, Kevin was ceremonially given the call sign Psych, for his last name is Ward. (Psych Ward; get it?) As Psych and I watched the new guys play silly pilot games and swap aviator "There I was stories," we laughed and understood why we loved our Air Force. As the ceremony came to a close, they invited Psych front and center for one last harrah. He toasted his Diet Dr. Pepper to the warriors of the Panther, Reapers, Tigers, and to all the others out there serving.

As we departed, he pulled aside a new B-2 instructor pilot and congratulated him for his superior performance during training. To his last hour, Psych mentored and built up those around him. As we drove home, he shared that he was happy leaving the Air Force unit in good hands. He looked forward to going home to his loving wife and daughters. In a matter of days, he would begin a new career as a pilot for Southwest Airlines. But today was one of those really good days, where he was able to reflect on a rewarding career filled with adventure and honor. I was fortunate to share this day with him, for it made me realize the importance of doing things right and finishing strong.

On the flip side of Psych's memorable bon voyage story, I have witnessed men who left their careers full of bitterness. I attended retirement ceremonies where retirees bad-mouthed others, and all for what? Bitterness destroys relationships and leaves bad memories. Have you ever watched a competitive game where someone gave it their all 99 percent of the time and then fell short at the end? Ever seen a football star fumble the ball in the Super Bowl? How about a soccer star missing a penalty shot in the World Cup final (please don't remind me—Italy vs. Brazil, 1994!). It's not fair that superstars will be remembered through time for how they finished that one game, but that's how it goes. Most people remember how you finish. So why not finish strong, especially if you control the show? Why speak ill of others or burn bridges? Stay positive. As you transition to new adventures, have that attitude of finishing strong. I know this from firsthand experience.

During my last day at work before retiring the first time, I stayed late to ensure everything was taken care of. I was in the training squadron late that night when the senior commander inadvertently stepped in, for he forgot his hat in one of the rooms. He asked why I was still at work when I was about to retire. I explained that I wanted to tie up all loose ends and that I would deeply miss our unit and mission.

Years later, the airline company I was working for unexpectedly declared bankruptcy after I had been there for just three months. My old commander asked if I would consider returning as a voluntary pilot recalled to active duty. He was looking for a few experienced B-2 stealth pilots to augment the force. It felt great knowing that the Air Force team wanted me back. My first instinct was to not return, for after the airline bankruptcy, I had taken a new job with a great salary. After watching a segment on the news depicting caskets being carried off a C-17 cargo aircraft, however, I realized that my nation was still at war and could use my skills one more time. I gladly accepted my nation's recall to active duty. Before I knew it, I had a B-2 stealth bomber strapped to my back again while serving as an Operations Officer supervising combat strikes.

I was asked to return likely due to my prior work ethic and how I finished. Had I left with bitterness or bad relations, then it would have been extremely unlikely that I would have been asked to return to the Air Force that I love.

Besides premeditating on what you will *say* during the transition to retirement, think about what you will *do* to shape future opportunities. Everyone should have the luxury of retiring once, only to be given an opportunity to return. During my second time around serving, my perspective was so different from the first. Isn't it amazing how we can forecast certain outcomes based on signs from the past! If the sky changes color and the temperature changes rapidly, then look out for the potential of thunderstorms. The key is awareness and foreknowledge. If you know that you will be retiring soon, then it is your responsibility to take certain actions to prepare yourself and your family for the future. This includes everything from common sense basics such as getting out of debt, to having an emergency fund in case you lose a job in the transition, all the way to building a quiver of resumes touting your various strengths to match certain job opportunities. Of great importance is meeting with your family to determine whether your new profession should be about money, location, or a specific job.

I strongly encourage all service members to maximize their educational benefits and get as many higher learning degrees as possible. Perhaps this may mean your spouse returning to school, making a career change, or joining the work force as well. Many companies looking for potential employees have minimum educational standards to meet the job requirement. By augmenting your professional skills with additional academic degrees and licenses, you will greatly increase your probability of being hired. Many professional organizations can assist you in marketing your military skills and properly changing the military jargon into language civilians understand.

Where you are currently in your career will shape what your desired end state will be. Allow me to encourage you to have an end state like that of Psych—one where you will look back and be proud of your service and respected by your coworkers, friends, and family. As you prepare for retirement or a significant transition, finish strong. Ideally you will be able to enjoy your fini–flight with members of your team and smile at the past as you position yourself for new horizons.

Heavenly Father, give me the strength of character to finish strong. Remove all forms of bitterness from my soul and fill my life with Your love.

HOW DO YOU SEE YOUR FINI-FLIGHT? Who do you envision surrounding you? What can you do now to make sure you finish strong?

Resources

See "Transitioning into a New Career" in appendix C.

TWENTY-NINE

Only Three Pizzas in the Freezer!

Preparing for Civilian Life

She has prepared a great banquet, mixed the wines, and set the table.

Proverbs 9:2,
New Living Translation

"Don't trouble yourself preparing for this dinner party. I've got it this time!" Tony assured me. He shared his intentions of inviting his Combined Air Operations Center (CAOC) over for a Christmas dinner party while we were stationed in Italy. Ninety-nine percent of the CAOC was made up of European military members. Learning new cultures intrigued me. I looked forward to an evening meeting new friends and sampling their authentic European dishes. Entertaining and cooking launch my endorphins into bliss; however, Tony wished to spare me preparing for a grandiose dinner party while I studied for my college finals.

Since I routinely organized the military dinner functions, Tony's initiative to "man the food" was a welcome change. His creative idea of asking couples to bring their favorite authentic dish from their country would reduce my workload and provide a great opportunity for everyone to sample each other's homeland recipes. Single military members would bring a beverage or dessert. Tony planned the dinner preparations perfectly—or so we thought. The lesson we learned that night will trail me into my grave.

Our annual family gingerbread house was baked, decorated, and sparkled with colorful blinking Christmas lights. Homemade sugar cookies scented the clean Italian condo. The kids and I set up the nativity scene my mom had purchased during her trip to Mexico. I restrained myself from preparing numerous dishes as I normally would. An uneasy feeling kept nagging at me, but I shrugged it off and continued grating cheese and chopping vegetables for my three appetizers. We eagerly awaited our guests. We were ready—but not for what was about to occur!

The first group of gregarious Italian soldiers arrived. All four of them were unmarried. They proudly handed me their select bottles of wine. They explained how two bottles came from their own family's vineyard. If you have visited or lived in Europe, you know that wine is to daily life as air is to breathing; you cannot separate the two. A knock on the door preceded three French officers who were also single. They gifted me with their special French vintages that supposedly no other country could surpass. Then our Spanish friends arrived. *Finally,* I thought, *a main course to go along with my three appetizers that were disappearing fast.* "Where's Judith?" I asked Carlos. "She is visiting her parents in Spain and will be back next week, but here, I want you to have the best wine from our homeland." I graciously thanked him as my clothes became dampened with a nervous sweat.

When Tony planned the dinner party, he did not realize that over two-thirds of those attending were single. As the room filled, so did our countertop with assorted beverages and only three main courses. Tony's Spanish commander and wife arrived, bringing a beautiful Paella dish. An American couple, whose roots stemmed back to Korea, brought a chicken and rice dish, and a Swedish unmarried female (bless her soul) brought the ingredients to make Swedish pancakes. These were wonderful dishes, but for the 35-plus hungry soldiers and a few scattered spouses, I might as well have given them a plate of ten beans and said, *"Abbondanza!"* Our scant amount of food for this anticipated banquet was definitely not the extravagant spread that Europeans are accustomed to.

I frantically searched for Tony, who was already keenly aware of our dilemma. He said, "Hurry, get the phone book! We'll call the local pizzeria and just have them deliver." The thought of pizzas catered to a room full of elegantly dressed Europeans was not only embarrassing but also offensive to a culture that boasts their love and compassion through the incredible preparation and vast display of food. Christmas parties were expected to surpass the normal extravagant dinner party by leaps and bounds. The worst part was that Europeans who had never visited the States thought this was how Americans celebrated!

I dialed the pizzeria. No answer. I dialed another restaurant, and then three more without answer. *Oh, no,* I thought. *Can this get any worse?* I then realized it was Wednesday, which is when the restaurants in our town took the day off. Now what? I was in panic mode. People were getting hungry but maintained agitated politeness. We jogged to our garage, one block from the house, where our freezer was located since it was too large to fit thorough our narrow Italian doorway. I found three frozen pizzas and some Bagel Bites that I had previously bought at the American army base commissary. We proceeded to cook them. We attempted to explain the mix-up concerning the food sign-up list, but in European cultures, sign-up lists are unheard of; the dinner host provides everything. Potlucks are as bizarre to Europeans as Italians taking a three-hour afternoon rest is unheard of in America. Regardless of our efforts to escape with some understanding, we knew this dinner party flop was unredeemable.

We muddled through the evening, trying to hold our heads high and making the best of the situation, but this incident tipped the humiliation scale over the top, especially when I would have loved to whip up some hickory-smoked beef brisket with homemade baked beans, marinated grilled salmon, and other specialty dishes. One of my favorite verses is "entertain strangers, for by doing so you may be entertaining angels" (Hebrews 13:2). I sure hoped that our guests were understanding angels that evening. Tony and I were so humiliated at our lack of preparedness that we couldn't even talk after the event, but we learned an incredible lesson: Preparation is the key to success.

Unforeseen situations in military life are guaranteed. Preparing for unexpected events beforehand will cushion the landing in case you find yourself in an unwanted situation. Whenever Tony and I see upcoming challenges such as TDYs, deployments, and retirements on the horizon, all we have to do is say, "Remember Italy," which is code for "Be prepared," and we know we need to saddle up for unforeseeable obstacles.

"Get ready!" retired military couples forewarned us. "You have no idea the shock your budget and lifestyle will have when you separate from the service." Therefore, we "remembered Italy" as we reduced our budget to pay down debt to ease the blow of decreased income. It's difficult to count on a steadfast health plan to fit your family needs as our nation faces health care and insurance changes. By preparing now, you'll be able to overcome potential obstacles and provide for your family.

Career changes strain not only finances but emotions as well. One minute you have a built-in military support group with couples facing the same challenges, and then the next day you wake up in Hopeulikit, Georgia (a real town by the way), with no commander's wife knocking on your door with a welcome pie in hand, inviting you to a slew of military functions. Many spouses that I know felt isolated after moving to a non-military community. They have to exert extra energy to create friendships.

If you know you will be exchanging fatigues for civvies, prepare in advance by planning to get involved with school, community, or church events to meet new friends.

Perhaps you and your warrior are contemplating separating from the military before retirement. Communication regarding work expectations is crucial. Both separating and retiring from the military may force spouses to make a career change or step into the working arena. A spouse's post-military expectations may be quite different from the warrior's. By battle-readying beforehand for what may occur two or three years down the road, you will lessen financial, emotional, and marital stress (see appendix A for a "Communication Tune-up for Couples").

When Tony retired the first time, we remained in a military community. After twenty years, I suddenly found myself back in the workforce as a school nurse. God graciously placed a dear friend, Lani, alongside me. Her husband had recently retired from the military as well. Talking about the drastic changes civilian life placed on our once-structured, secure military life was therapeutic. Although going through similar separation circumstances alongside a former military spouse is normally not the case, finding a trusted friend to confide in while facing transitions definitely lightens the emotional stress and takes the weight off your spouse's shoulders.

Remember Italy. Prepare now for upcoming transitions. Pray for God to help guide your upcoming decisions, even though they may be years down the road. Evaluate the changes your future transition presents before you're frantically dialing pizzerias for emergency help and discover that they are closed. Communicate your expectations with your spouse. Cushion your change by involving yourself in school, community, and church activities to meet new friends, and confide your emotions to a trusted friend. Don't be stuck with only three frozen pizzas when your life can be a smorgasbord of wonderful opportunities!

Dear Lord, thank You for the opportunity to serve this great country. Help us take the lessons gleaned from military life and smoothly transition into our next adventure. Direct our path as we prepare for the future.

IF YOU COULD CHOOSE ANY PROFESSION, what would it be? What amount of education, finances, or time will it require to achieve this goal? What preparations have you made in the event an expected or unexpected career change occurs? Do you have funds set aside for family and/or medical emergencies, and college savings for children?

Resources

Check the "Transitioning into a New Career" section in appendix C for websites to help ready both spouses and warriors for reintegration into civilian life.

THIRTY

Just a Cup of Coffee

Showing Appreciation to Our Warriors

*If anyone has material possessions and sees his brother in
need but has no pity on him, how can the love of God be
in him? Dear children, let us not love with words or tongue
but with actions and in truth.*

1 John 3:17–18,
NIV (1984)

Just a cup of coffee. That's all it took to plant wide grins on the som-
ber faces of two army soldiers who walked into McDonald's near
Fort Riley, Kansas. My daughter and I had stopped midway through
Kansas for breakfast on our way to Colorado. Two serious-looking
young men stepped behind us in line. After paying for our food, I
placed a twenty on the counter and quietly asked the cashier to buy
breakfast for the two young men in fatigues and tell them, "Thank
you for serving our country." From our table, I glanced across the

room and located the two men, now glowing with a newfound cheerfulness. Some stranger appreciated their service.

During the Vietnam War, I was a young child, but I learned about the unjust, neglected welcome our returning veterans received when I was older. That episode sadly stains our history books. America has learned from its past mistakes, and I hope we will *never* allow those atrocities to repeat themselves, regardless of political beliefs. As I remember the two Fort Riley soldiers, I smile inside. These young men felt valued through a simple breakfast gesture; I felt like my tiny act somehow encompassed the Vietnam vets before me who never received that cup of coffee. My daughter was as delighted as I was, and I could see in her eyes the respect growing for our military heroes who selflessly serve this country.

I've gathered some true accounts from real people who have witnessed or received gratitude in the form of actions from others. I'd like to share the kindness bestowed upon them so these actions can be emulated. We honor each of you who serves as active duty combat warriors, dependent spouses and children, and military parents who release your treasured sons and daughters into the hands of God when they sign the dotted line. Thanks will never be enough. These gestures honor *all* our veterans and families who serve our country—past and present. And to our brave Vietnam veterans—*Welcome home*. This overdue cup of coffee's for you.

Ladies' Day
Kassandra

"There have been numerous times when people in a shopping line let me go in front of them because I'm in uniform, and they say, 'Thank you for your service . . . ' While I was on TDY at Keesler Air Force Base, Mississippi, ten of us went out to lunch. Sitting at the table next to us was a group of ladies. Right before they left, they thanked us for serving and gave money to one of my classmates to pay for our lunch. Once they left, we counted the money and between eight women, they gave $120."

Off-Duty Kindness
Chuck

"It was a no-brainer," Sheriff Chuck Heiss said. "You don't think about it. You just know it's the right thing to do, and you do it." Chuck was off the clock the day he came across a distraught woman on the side of a busy Missouri highway. Her car had blown a tire, and she was a hundred miles from the airport where she was to pick up her husband returning from Afghanistan. Chuck's kindness transformed an otherwise devastating day into a joyful reunion. Not only did he drive three hours on his day off to reunite an Air Force spouse with her husband at the exact moment he walked out the gate, but he also contacted the base commander and arranged for the car to be fixed and towed back to Whiteman Air Force Base before the couple returned. To ice the reunion cake, Sheriff Heiss pulled into the couple's driveway with police lights shining to surprise their unsuspecting kids. On that memorable day, a terribly missed daddy hopped out from a police car's back seat and reunited with his family. Sheriff Heiss' kindness imprints this family's heart, and their story will surely be passed down for generations to come.

A "Guardian Angel"
Shawnelle

"During our first deployment, I was nineteen years old and a first-time mom with a six-month-old son. I was new to the military world. It was my first time away from home, and I was losing my mind. I would catch myself crying because I knew what was expected of me, but I wasn't sure how to handle anything. One day I took my son to the park and sat there while he slept in his stroller. I was thinking about my husband and how I wished he were with me to help me adjust. I knew it was selfish, but I'd only been a military wife for four months, and I wasn't sure about anything. A woman sat down next to me. She said, 'I can tell you are confused and lost. It's written all over your face. It's okay to be both of those things for our job as military wives is not easy. Our husbands put their lives on the line, not just for our country, but for us, as well. I am sure he would rather be here with you, but right now he's making sure you are always free. Dry your tears, hug your baby, and remember that you are a military spouse because God knows you are strong.' She walked away and left me with so much to think about. I felt so much better, and right then I realized what it was to be a military spouse. Now and then I see a new military wife with that same look on her face, so I share the same wisdom I once was given. It was more than just kindness from another military wife, it was a guardian angel I had that day whom God knew I needed."

Sheer Caring
L. Dawn

"My husband had already been gone TAD[21] for nine months when we got PCS[22] orders to move, and then he deployed immediately for another seven months as soon as we moved from overseas back to the States. There was barely time to unpack, much less decorate. Our five kids and I were having a difficult time adjusting to our new home without my husband, and I was dealing with some serious medical issues of my own while helping our disabled child settle into a new school. I wistfully thought that some personal touches like curtains and wall hangings might make our house feel more like a 'home,' but I simply didn't have time for anything but the necessities.

"Before Christmas, I found a flyer on our door from a local church's military outreach program, offering a choice of help with painting, yard work, hanging pictures, or curtains. I was so touched, I sat down and cried just reading the flyer. I was so humbled that complete strangers would volunteer to spend their Saturday afternoon during a busy holiday season to help my family have those nice little 'extras,' no strings attached. During those months when my husband was deployed and my children and I were adjusting to a new town where we often felt alone, every time I felt down, I noticed those curtains and was reminded that someone cared."

---

21. Temporary assigned duty.
22. Permanent change of station. Basically, orders to relocate.

Caffeine Kindness and Delta Compassion
Cathy

"A few days after my son, Steven, returned home, he met me at my office in uniform and we went out to lunch. I noticed one of the other patrons, a man in a nice suit, watching us as we looked at the gift shop's mugs and bags of coffee. Steven chose a coffee mug to purchase and also ordered two coffees to go. As he pulled out his wallet, the man moved quickly to block him and said 'I've got this.' He paid for all our stuff and thanked Steven for his service. He handed Steven his business card and said, 'If you ever need a job, call me.' He's a local business owner."

"On a different occasion, a kind Delta manager bent a few rules to allow our entire family to accompany Steven to his gate the night he left for Belgium. We sat with him and helped settle his nerves a little, and when his flight was called to board, we put our hands on him right there and prayed for him. It meant *so much* to have those last few moments with him. (Thank you, Delta! Also, thanks for boarding all the military passengers first!)"

Something to Chew On
Dolores

"I flew to spend time with my son before his deployment. We were at the public market in Seattle on Veterans Day. One vendor gave him a bag of gum and told him she always gives soldiers bags of it and tells them to send the wrappers back to let her know they are safe."

Donating Dad
Penny

"The medical technicians' faces light up as they see my dad's car pull into the parking lot. Nearly every month for the past twenty years my dad has treated this staff to his famous homemade pizza while he donates platelets at the neighborhood blood donation center.

"I've always been proud of my father selflessly donating, but when my army soldier son showed up in the ER with a life-threatening condition and received five units of platelets, I realized how donors like my dad saved my son's life. My father is an Army/Marine veteran and now serves as an Honor Guard volunteer who has performed ceremonies at 97 veterans' funerals, and he is a man of great faith. Recently, he described how Christians have become pew couch potatoes and how 'faith by itself, if it is not accompanied by action, is dead' (James 2:17). Recently, he challenged every congregation member in his town to put their faith into action. When sending a card to a military service member stating that you are praying for him or her, include that you donated plasma, platelets, or blood in their name for our wounded warriors. How much more would that mean? A gift of platelets, plasma, or blood can save numerous lives, from individuals fighting cancer to soldiers injured from IEDs while fighting for their country. Thanks, Dad, for saving lives and inspiring me and others to put feet on our faith. I love you."

Unexpected Wedding Presents
Tammy

"My son got married May 5, which was also my husband and my twentieth anniversary. After the wedding, we went to a local restaurant. My son was in his Class As (service dress uniform) and his wife was still in her wedding dress. We ordered, ate, and as we were about to ask for our check, the waitress told us that the meal had been paid for, and then she handed us four additional gift cards including four meals each! Apparently, four separate tables had offered to pay for our meal. The cashier told them someone had already paid, but the people said, 'Then we'll put it on a gift card.' We have since returned the favors by passing on those four gift cards to other military members we see in the restaurant. Also, while my son returned to his base from Dallas-Fort Worth, he was waiting in line to go through security, and every single person (approximately twenty) stepped aside and let him go to the front of the line."

A Tie-in with Tynan
Debi

"My son, Marco, called home to tell us that he lost both his legs the day before by a two hundred-pound IED and that he was on his way to Walter Reed Hospital in Bethesda, Maryland. After a week, my husband and I left Marco in the care of his loving wife and took the Metro to DC for the day. I sat next to a lady and her husband and, of course, started talking about my hero son. She wanted to know if it would be okay to get my son's address and mail him a card.

Well, of course. How nice. She told her parents about my son. Her parents told their friends about my son. A friend of the parents, Dr. Scott, heard Marco's story and was touched. My son reminded him of an Irish tenor, Dr. Ronan Tynan, who lost his legs at about the same age as Marco and is now a medical doctor, set fourteen world records in the Paralympics, has performed on Broadway, makes TV appearances, and the list goes on. Dr. Scott tracked down Dr. Tynan in Ireland, had him autograph two of his CDs, and sent them to my son, along with Dr. Tynan's biography hoping to inspire him. And it surely has. We will be forever grateful for his act of kindness."

Bumped into First Class
Anna

"When I was coming home from Afghanistan with three other soldiers for emergency reasons, we boarded last because we had just gotten off standby. We were spread throughout the cabin. The captain made an announcement before he left the gate that he was proud to be transporting four Purple Heart recipients that day. We got a standing ovation from the whole plane. About ten minutes before we left the gate, the flight attendants approached all four of us and asked us to retrieve our personal belongings. We figured we had been bumped off the flight, but to our amazement, four businessmen offered their seats in First Class to us, and they took the ride home in coach. We were shocked and amazed that we were treated like royalty; all we did was our job, but it was nice to see that someone, somewhere, appreciates what we do."

Thank You for Serving
Brie

"We were at Branson Landing, Missouri, shopping. My brother, Antonio, and I were sitting on a bench waiting for my mom's shopping high to end. Antonio was not in uniform, but that didn't stop an adorable little boy, probably about ten years old, who was fully decked out in oversized camo shorts, combat boots, army hat, and shirt, from identifying my brother as a soldier. He approached Antonio and asked if he served in the military. He then said, 'Thank you for serving, sir,' and saluted Antonio. This act made the Top 10 sweetest moments I've ever encountered. I don't think anyone could have reassured my brother more at that moment of his decision to serve, or made him happier and feeling more appreciated."

Anniversary Surprise
Angelle

"For our tenth anniversary we decided to celebrate as a family at Disney World. We saved up and off we went with our children, who were five and three years old at the time. On our final night there, my husband, Paul, and I decided to have a date night to celebrate at a very nice five-star restaurant, the Grand Floridian Hotel. It was a great night celebrating *us*. During the course of dinner, our waiter asked where we lived and what we did. At the end of a very long enjoyable time, Paul went to take care of the bill. I came from the bathroom to see Paul standing by the hostess booth looking very puzzled. I asked what was wrong. He said, 'You are not going to believe this! Someone in the restaurant overheard me saying I was in the military and paid for our meal!' I was in shock also. You see, our bill was over $300. We knew it was going to be big. We chose to celebrate here and had saved up for the meal. The restaurant employee would only tell us that the person who purchased our dinner wanted to remain anonymous. He had even paid a generous tip. To this day we do not know who this person was but we are very humbled and grateful. I can't tell the story without tearing up!"

Healing Time
Phil

"I joined the Marine Corps shortly after the war in 'Nam ended. Let's just say the public was not kind to us. Over this last year I experienced something new; a person said, 'Thank you for your service.' I did not know what to say. My daughter, now serving in the US Army, said it was because I was wearing my Order of the Purple Heart cap. Later that month, we were at a small town rodeo and the MC asked that all vets stand up. Again, I was shocked to hear people clap and be thankful for the blood we left in the sand. I guess the point of this story is simple . . . a thank you goes a long way. If I had been given that kind of support before . . . wow . . . the healing would have been better and I think it would have been faster. Now that my daughter serves, I make sure she knows she is appreciated and respected."

"We should not look back unless it is to derive useful lessons from past errors, and for the purpose of profiting by dearly bought experience." —George Washington

Dear Lord, let me never take the sacrifices that our military men and women make to protect our freedom for granted. Give me reminders to pray for our military families every day, and open the door for opportunities to show our warriors my appreciation.

WHAT ARE YOU DOING to show military families that you care about them and appreciate their service? Does your church offer any ministries for military families that you could join? If not, why not start one yourself? Do you know a military family that could use a night out while you babysit? Are you a business owner? Show your gratitude to our men and women in uniform by hiring them. Check the appendixes for more ideas about how to help support our troops and their families. Just a cup of coffee or a simple thank you goes a long way.

Communication Tune-Up for Couples

Remove the dross from the silver, and a silversmith can produce a vessel.

Proverbs 25:4

Deployments add stress to military relationships. Surprised? Of course not. Statistics show that 30,000 military marriages ended in 2011, leading to the highest divorce rate for military couples in ten years.[23] The number-one issue deployed service members worry about is how they'll communicate during the separation about finances, child care, family decisions, and other important topics.[24] Before deployments (or during them, if you are already in the midst of one), take time to fill out the following communication tune-up. Hear each other's heart while discussing these relationship issues.

23. Michelle Miller, "Trouble on the Home Front—Military Divorces on the Rise." *CBS News*, 5 August 2012, http://www.cbsnews.com/8301-505263_162 -57474778/trouble-on-the-home-front-military-divorces-on-the-rise/.
24. Sarah J. Schmidt, "Military Family Finances: Surviving the Financial Stress of Deployment," *Military Money*, 14 March 2012, http://www.militarymoney.com/ MilitaryLife/deployment/tabid/109/itemId/2241/Default.aspx.

To begin, pray together. If you are uncomfortable, just read the following words out loud: "Lord, you already know the threats that can harm our relationship. Please help us gently express our honest feelings about the following topics without becoming angry or upset. Make us into a couple that can withstand the fires that separations often ignite."

Here are some helpful basic rules of engagement:

- Take equal turns discussing each topic.
- Remain quiet while the other person answers the question. It's important for you to listen—*really* listen. (A method that works in our home is for the listening spouse to take notes to avoid forgetting questions.) Input can be given after both have expressed their thoughts.
- Take a fifteen-minute break if you hit a communication wall. If you need a longer break, reconvene at a designated time. Remain committed to tackling the issues.
- Write your answers separately—no designated secretary.
- After you've worked through the questionnaire with your spouse, combine your answers in a journal or on your computer and make two copies to keep for reminders and encouragement in case the relational stressors surface during separation.

O

LONELINESS

> *So do not fear, for I am with you; do not be dismayed, for I am your God. I will strengthen you and help you; I will uphold you with my righteous right hand.*
>
> Isaiah 41:10

1. What types of social gatherings interest you (i.e., neighborhood picnic, church event, parenting groups, sports teams, dancing)? How does your spouse feel about you attending these functions? Do these functions provide positive support? How?
2. Who is a good friend who positively influences you that you can spend time with during the separation?
3. How do you feel about opposite sex friendships? What is acceptable?
4. Many affairs begin due to loneliness. What will you do if someone of the opposite sex begins to show you attention?
5. What Bible verse can you both memorize to strengthen you when loneliness or temptation sets in?

O

PORNOGRAPHY AND SOCIAL NETWORKS

I will set nothing wicked before my eyes.

Psalm 101:3,
New King James Version

According to a survey of 1,600 top divorce lawyers, more than half of all military divorces involved a spouse hooked on pornography.[25] A 2010 survey by the American Academy of Matrimonial Lawyers showed that 81 percent of the nation's top divorce attorneys

---

25. Jon R. Anderson, "Addicted to Online Porn," *Army Times*, 31 March 2010.

reported an increase in social networking websites being used as evidence in divorce cases. Facebook is the leader, being cited in 66 percent of cases that involve online evidence.[26] K. Jason, coauthor of *Facebook and Your Marriage,* stated, "Office romances and out-of-town trysts can take months or even years to develop. Affairs happen with a lightning speed on Facebook. It puts temptation in the path of people who would never in a million years risk having an affair."[27]

1. What are your feelings about social networks like Facebook?
2. How does your spouse feel about you having opposite sex friendships on the Internet? What is acceptable?
3. What is your plan if friends share pornographic material or erotica?
4. What actions will you proactively take to avoid becoming tempted with pornography, erotica websites, Facebook attractions, etc.?

O

ONENESS VERSUS ISOLATION

The two are united into one.

Mark 10:8,
New Living Translation

26. Michael Foust, "Facebook Divorce Stats: Couples 'Be Wise,' Experts Say," *Crosswalk.com*, 14 April 2012, http://www.crosswalk.com/family/marriage/divorce-and-remarriage/facebook-divorce-stats-couples-be-wise-experts-say.html.
27. K. Jason and Kelli Krafsky, *Facebook and Your Marriage* (Maple Valley, WA: Turn the Tide Resources Group, 2010).

Oneness occurs when both partners work toward common goals. You encourage one another to succeed and are involved with each other's daily progress. Whether you support the other in raising a family or realizing career ambitions, you are tuned in to the other's life, and your actions convey that support.

Isolation occurs when partners act independently of each other and don't communicate desires and ambitions. Goals become *me*-focused rather than *we*-focused. You move away from each other gradually and lose touch with what is happening in each other's lives. This often occurs in deployments because of communication neglect, the need to become self-sufficient, and the physical distance separating couples. When the deployed partners reunite, they are surprised to find they don't have much in common anymore. Conveying personal and family goals before and during deployments keeps your relationship focused on oneness. Otherwise, you will likely isolate yourselves, and your relational journey will need repair.

1. What are your personal goals for family, work, career, and/or education during this deployment? Do you feel you have your spouse's support in these areas?
2. How can you best support your spouse's ambitions? What actions will help the other most?
3. What devotional or marriage-strengthening book would you like to read together while separated? (See appendix C for relationship-strengthening books.)

O

BECOMING OVERWHELMED

> *Do not be anxious about anything, but in every situation,*
> *by prayer and petition, with thanksgiving, present your*
> *requests to God. And the peace of God, which transcends*
> *all understanding, will guard your hearts and your minds*
> *in Christ Jesus.*
>
> *Philippians 4:6–7*

There comes a time in every deployment when the home-front spouse could use a helping hand. Requesting support does not equal weakness; a visit from a family member, friend, or church support person rejuvenates an overwhelmed spouse. A child may become injured, ill, or have challenges due to the separation, a parent or relative may need additional support, holiday blues can set in, or just the accumulated daily stresses may become overwhelming. Planning for additional support now removes the stress of finding help later or during a crisis. Also, plan to touch base with your chaplain or local pastor as a couple before the deployment. This will make you both feel more comfortable if you need to call upon him later.

1. If an emergency occurs, what family member will you call upon for support?
2. Is there a family member or friend willing to visit to help "give a breather" to the home-front spouse? If so, does this person need financial help to travel? What amount can you

set aside monthly to assist such a helper? Have you already contacted the person to make arrangements?

3. What church or community support is available?

○

CHILDREN'S DISCIPLINE

For the moment all discipline seems painful rather than pleasant, but later it yields the peaceful fruit of righteousness to those who have been trained by it.

Hebrews 12:11,
English Standard Version

Agreeing on discipline issues before and during separations strengthens families. Guilt that one parent (or both in some cases) is absent, especially during pivotal events such as recitals, sports events, holidays, or graduations often causes parents to overindulge and give in to their child's every want. Children can become masters of parent manipulation, causing undue stress in relationships. Pre-adolescents and teens may act out to get extra attention while a parent is deployed, or they may become isolated and depressed. Deciding beforehand how to discipline and handle parenting challenges together, even while apart, conveys strength and unity to a child and provides needed security. If you are a single military parent, applicable questions can be used with your caregiver.

1. How would you like to communicate discipline issues while separated? (Remember, after Skyping, e-mailing, or phoning, the warrior returns to the mission and must stay single-minded to remain safe.)

2. Would you prefer to discuss non-emergency parenting challenges as they come up or during a specific time of the week? What method of communication would be best— e-mail, Skype, etc.?

3. What community, church, and military support organizations are available to give breaks to the home-front spouse?

4. Children of Reservists and National Guard members may feel isolated. If their school is not near a military installation, it is likely none of their friends understand military challenges of having a deployed parent. Each military branch's installation offers a Family Readiness Center, which provides various family support programs and social events for military children. Tri-care allows for dependents to receive counseling sessions from a provider without a referral. What support programs are available to help your children cope with deployment?

O

FINANCES

"But don't begin until you count the cost. For who would begin construction of a building without first calculating the cost to see if there is enough money to finish it? Otherwise,

> *you might complete only the foundation before running out of money."*
>
> Luke 14:28–30,
> New Living Translation

Financial stress is a huge contributor to marital crashes. The *New York Times* noted that "couples who reported disagreeing about finance once a week were over 30 percent more likely to get divorced than couples who reported disagreeing about finances a few times a month."[28] Reduce financial stress by communicating how you will manage finances and spending habits during and after deployments *before* separating, if orders allow. Numerous veterans return from deployments to find their finances in shambles, and many home-front spouses have sunk into tremendous debt when their spouse returns and goes on an emotional shopping spree. (Emotional spending commonly occurs the first two months after deployment and the first two months after the deployed member returns home. Families fall into debt shortly after the deployed member returned because they "spent a lot of money trying to make up for lost time."[29]) Create a budget and discuss spending plans now to avoid those financial potholes, which cause relationship collisions. See appendix C for resources to help you as you plan.

---

28. Catherine Rampell, "Money Fights Predict Divorce Rates," *New York Times*, 17 December 2009.

29. Sarah J. Schmidt, "Military Family Finances: Surviving the Financial Stress of Deployments." *Military Money*, 2004, http://www.militarymoney.com/Military Life/deployment/tabid/109/itemId/2241/Default.aspx.

1. Have you drawn up an agreeable budget for this deployment? If not, by what date can you have one ready?
2. Many couples find they have completely different ideas about spending combat pay. The warrior returns and buys a motorcycle while the home-front spouse plans to deposit the money into the children's college fund. How do you want to spend the extra income?

○

HOMECOMING EXPECTATIONS

And let us consider how we may spur one another on toward love and good deeds, not giving up meeting together, as some are in the habit of doing, but encouraging one another—and all the more as you see the Day approaching.

Hebrews 10:24–25

Homecoming expectations may change as the deployment progresses. Discuss what you would like to do as a family and individually after returning home. Reevaluate these plans at different deployment intervals to remain on the same page.

1. What are your homecoming plans right now, prior to deployment?
2. Schedule a date for halfway through deployment to discuss whether your homecoming plans have changed.

3. A week prior to returning home, discuss any additional changes to your homecoming plans.

○

PREPARE—JUST IN CASE

USAA.com makes preparing for the unlikely event of death easy. After you arrive at the site, click on the tab "Advice Center," and then "Deployment" under the "Military Life" heading. Next click "Preparing for Deployment." You will discover how to get your legal affairs in order, including how to create a will, power of attorney, and joint accounts. There is also a helpful deployment checklist, and insurance and finance information, as well.

○

Communicating will strengthen your relationship to withstand military challenges; however, once in a while, you may need professional help. If you have not made headway while discussing these issues, seek counseling. For more information or to find a counselor, see appendix C.

Invest in your relationship. Once you have worked through these issues, either as a couple or with a counselor, your relationship will be richer and fuller as God intended.

Combat-Related Stress Helps

He reached down from on high and took hold of me; he drew me out of deep waters. He rescued me from my powerful enemy, from my foes, who were too strong for me.

Psalm 18:16–17

It's unfathomable to think of plopping a soldier in the middle of the combat zone without going through the rigors of boot camp that transform him or her into a warrior. In training the service member learns about weapon proficiency, honor through service, how to fight the enemy, and the importance of a battle buddy, among other things. Just as we would never send a civilian to the war zone without boot camp, we cannot take that highly trained warrior from the combat zone and drop him back into civilian and family life without equipping him and family members with tools to successfully transition. The following resources arm warriors, parents, spouses, family members, and friends with the necessary education and crucial tools to successfully transition from the combat zone to family and civilian life.

The statistics about combat-related stress are sobering, but education is key to healing. Addressing the challenges head-on with tools to heal war's invisible wounds and inviting God into the transition process restores hope for our military veterans and imparts not only hope, but also victory. If you are currently experiencing post-traumatic stress (PTS), also known as combat operational stress or post-traumatic stress disorder (PTSD),[30] you have battle buddies at your side, experiencing your same emotions. *Choose* to heal, and explore the restoration path that is right for you and your loved one. You are not alone; there is an ultimate battle buddy waiting for your call.

The National Center for PTSD reports that 40 percent of those who've fought in Afghanistan or Iraq have or will acquire this disorder. Because the warrior feels he does not fit into home or civilian life and no one can understand his or her emotions, the warrior often wants to redeploy. He doesn't love his family any less; he just is poorly prepared to readjust. Depression can result from feeling out of control. In worst cases, veterans become suicidal. There are now more deaths by suicide than the total number

---

30. PTSD is an anxiety disorder induced by experiencing or witnessing a traumatic event. The afflicted person recalls the event's trauma as if it were currently happening. Symptoms may include—but are not limited to—emotional numbing, sleep problems, flashbacks, irritability, hyper vigilance, depression, anxiety, isolation, and poor concentration or memory. Symptoms usually appear within the first three months of the traumatic event, but may be delayed for years. For a diagnosis, two or more symptoms must last more than thirty days and cause significant distress or impairment of daily life. One can have all the symptoms, but if they're not disrupting daily life activities, then the person is diagnosed with post-traumatic stress (PTS), but not the disorder.

of soldiers killed in Afghanistan and Iraq since those wars began.[31] Statistics for 2010 report eighteen military veterans commit suicide per day.[32] The use of prescription drugs—pain medication, antidepressants, sleeping pills, and even an epilepsy medicine—to treat PTSD has grown by 62 percent to 400 percent since the Iraq War began.[33]

Transitioning back to civilian life adds a new dimension to combat-related stress for the Reserve and National Guard veterans. Unlike active duty members, civilian coworkers don't relate to veterans' experiences, and warriors feel isolated. Reserve and National Guard members return to civilian jobs where emphases on trivial matters, such as completing reports, outshine the serious reality of combat. More and more Reserve veterans are requesting to redeploy where they feel they "fit in." Marriages and job security suffers, and in worst cases, veterans become suicidal.

The stigma of receiving professional help prevents many warriors from seeking help. A 2004 Walter Reed Research Center Survey showed that 60 percent of veterans felt other military members would have less confidence in them if they were to seek help, 63

31. Nicholas D. Kristof, "A Veteran's Death, the Nation's Shame," New York Times Sunday Review, *New York Times*, 13 June 2012, http://www.nytimes.com/2012/04/15/opinion/sunday/kristof-a-veterans-death-the-nations-shame.html?_r=1.

32. Rick Maze, "18 Veterans Commit Suicide Each Day," *Army Times*, 22 November 2011, http://www.armytimes.com/news/2010/04/military_veterans_suicide_042210w/.

33. David Ollinger and Erin Emery, "The Battle Within: Soldiering On in Pain," *Denver Post*, 3 April 2012, http://www.denverpost.com/thebattlewithin/ci_10302647#ixzz23A1z8zRB.

percent felt leadership would treat them differently, and 65 percent felt leadership would blame them (feelings of shame).[34]

As bleak as these statistics may seem, there is hope and healing and veterans are triumphing over combat-related stress. One key element is being able to relate with fellow veterans tackling the same challenges. Make the choice to prepare for a potential battle and heal if you're in the midst of one. Preparation and restoration is now your new mission. The following organizations can provide help. All the following support resources are also available at www.called toserveministry.com.

DNA Military

www.dnamilitary.org. This organization provides mission-critical military care to our nation's warriors, families, leaders, and caregivers through training, services, and resources, which promote resiliency and relational health throughout the deployment cycle. These services include retreats, counseling professionals, and print and media resources.

International Hyperbaric Medical Foundation

www.hyperbaricmedicalfoundation.org. A cutting-edge treatment that is headlining the PTSD success charts is hyperbaric oxygen therapy (HBOT). Statics show that HBOT is eliminating depression by 51 percent, reducing headaches by 87 percent, and reducing other PTSD symptoms by 30 percent. HBOT treatments are offered

---

34. Charles W. Hoge and Carl A. Castro, "Impact of Combat Duty in Iraq and Afghanistan, Mental Health Problems, and Barriers to Care," *The New England Journal of Medicine*, 2005.

nationwide (http://www.hyperbaricmedicalfoundation.org/Treat ment.html) and a grant is available for those veterans qualified for treatment (www.nbirr.org). Consult with your doctor about this treatment.

Liberty University's (LU) Institute for Military Resilience (IMR) Online

http://www.luonline.com/military-students/institute-military -resilience/. This program is pioneering a path to PTSD recovery and successfully healing military families and caregivers nationwide. While receiving professional guidance from PTSD experts, veterans also receive college credits, and PTSD care remains confidential. Major General Bob Dees (US Army, Ret.), director of IMR, states, "In light of the daunting mental and behavioral health trends in our military, we absolutely must get everything in the fight, including help, hope, healing, and resilience through the power of faith. The IMR is the nation's first faith-based resilience program for veterans, troops, and military families; as well as those who provide care and counsel for them."

Make the Connection

www.maketheconnection.net. This site connects veterans and their friends and family members with information, resources, and solutions to relevant issues affecting their lives. This is a superb, informative site that gives veterans and family members guidelines on how triumph over military-related challenges.

Not Alone

www.notalone.com. Not Alone provides programs, services, and resources for warriors, veterans, and families. A variety of programs are offered for warriors and family, both online and offline. Not Alone also offers a social network on your profile page that allows you to connect and interact with others experiencing life after war.

PTSD Foundation of America

www.ptsdusa.net. This organization's mission is to bring healing to our military community through pastoral counseling and peer mentoring, both on an individual basis and in group settings. The number for their veteran crisis line is 1–800–273–TALK (8255). Veterans press "1."

Veteran's Caregiver Support

www.caregiver.va.gov. The Veteran's Administration knows your focus as a family caregiver is taking care of the veteran you love. It can be an incredibly demanding job, but you don't have to do it alone. This website will help you learn more about the support and services the VA offers family caregivers.

Wingman Project

www.wingmanproject.org. This organization was developed by the Air National Guard to help military veterans combat the very real enemy of hopelessness. The ACE training video, although made for airmen, will help anyone experiencing the feeling of hopelessness, and it provides steps for family members or friends to help their loved ones.

Recommended Combat Stress Healing Books

- *Once a Warrior: Wired for Life* by Bridget C. Cantrell and Chuck Dean. The authors show how to assist military personnel in utilizing their tremendous potential in achieving success and happiness after military service. This book highlights the transition from warrior to civilian. A workbook is also available.

- *Down Range: To Iraq and Back* by Bridget C. Cantrell and Chuck Dean. This vital information and resource manual is for both returning troops and their loved ones. Here you will find answers, explanations, and insights as to why so many combat veterans suffer from flashbacks, depression, fits of rage, nightmares, anxiety, emotional numbing, and other troubling aspects of PTSD.

- *Souls Under Siege: The Effects of Multiple Troop Deployments—and How to Weather the Storm* by Bridget C. Cantrell. This resource shows ways to support those living with the pressures of multiple deployments. It not only expands awareness of the issues involved, but outlines sensible tools for finding relief. This book will become a useful guide to be used over and over again.

- *The Combat Trauma Healing Manual: Christ-centered Solutions for Combat Trauma* by Nate Self.

- *When War Comes Home: Christ-Centered Healing for Wives of Combat Veterans* by Chris Adsit, Rahnella Adsit, and Marshele Carter Waddell. This book offers spiritual comfort and practical, Christ-centered solutions for wives of combat veterans struggling with the hidden wounds of war ranging from reintegration challenges to PTSD. Includes PTS, PTSD, and TBI treatments.

- *Wounded Warrior, Wounded Home* by Marshele Carter Waddell and Kelly K. Orr. This resource gives hurting families a look inside the minds and hearts of their wounded warriors and guides them in developing plans for physical, emotional, and spiritual wholeness in the wake of war.

Additional Resources

For all the following support resources and more, go to www.called toserveministry.com.

Daily Devotionals

- *Called to Serve: Encouragement, Support, and Inspiration for Military Families* by Lt. Colonel Tony (USAF, Ret.) and Penny Monetti. Our book identifies the top stressors soldiers and their loved ones face and offers thirty encouraging, biblically based readings to help couples combat relational threats.

- *Everybody's Breaking Pieces Off of Me* by Susan Lenzkes. If you or someone you know is struggling to balance the demands of work, marriage, parenthood, church, and community with the desire to live a godly life, then this book is for you!

- *Faith Deployed* and *Faith Deployed Again: Daily Encouragement for Military Wives* by Jocelyn Green. These collections of devotions squarely address the challenges wives face when their husbands are away protecting freedom.

- *Military Wives' New Testament with Psalms and Proverbs* by Jocelyn Green. Includes ninety special devotions written by military wives.

- *Our Daily Bread* from RBC Ministries. Devotional thoughts published in *Our Daily Bread* help readers spend time each day in God's Word. Monthly mailings are free! Visit odb.org.
- *Streams in the Desert: An Updated Edition in Today's Language* by L. B. Cowman. This devotional is filled with insight into the richness of God's provision and the purpose of His plan.

Bible Studies

- **Bible Study Fellowship** (www.bsfinternational.org). What began more than fifty years ago as a desire of a small group of women to deepen their faith through a weekly Bible study now includes men, women, and children around the world— all with that same desire. Locate a class at http://preview.bsf international.org/locate-a-class. What I loved about this study is that my children simultaneously studied the same topics I did. We were able to discuss them together.
- *For Men:* **Life of Valor** (www.lifeofvalor.com). Life of Valor is a resource that has been created by Navy SEALs for men who want to live more honorable lives. The SEALs that protect our country live by a code. This resource will challenge you to create your own code and apply it to your life.
- *For Women:* **Protestant Women of the Chapel** (www.pwoc .org). This military organization connects spouses wanting to further their Christian walk with other military members. Visit the site to find a chapter in your area.

Marriage Strengthening Books and Devotionals

- *The Five Love Languages* by Gary Chapman. Once you know your "love language," you'll understand why some attempts at romance work while others fall flat.

- *His Needs Her Needs: Building and Affair Proof Marriage* by William F. Harley Jr. A great tool to help couples discover each other's relational needs.

- *Man in the Mirror Edition: For Busy Couples Who Want More Intimacy in Their Relationships* by Patrick Morley. These 120 devotional readings will help you apply biblical truths to deepen your relationship, communicate better, understand each other, learn about what pulls you apart and how to stay together, raise your children, and share a future.

- *Operation Military Family: How Military Couples Are Fighting to Preserve Their Marriages* by Mike Schindler. A look at how others have successfully navigated deployments and transitioned back to civilian or post-deployment life.

- *Sex Begins in the Kitchen* by Dr. Kevin Leman. Dr. Kevin Leman explains how sexual intimacy is an expression of the care you and your spouse show each other in all areas of life.

- *Sheet Music: Uncovering the Secrets of Sexual Intimacy in Marriage* by Dr. Kevin Leman. Sex is about the quality of your entire love life. This book will expand and challenge your thinking, help you start your marriage off right, or go from humdrum to exciting if you're already married.

- *Stay in the Boat* by Linda W. Rook. This book provides the emotional and spiritual strength to help a woman sort through her confusion when her marriage is in trouble.
- *We All Married Idiots: Three Things You Will Never Change About Your Marriage and Ten Things You Can* by Elaine Miller. This book is a must for your relational toolbox. Tony and I have grown closer to God and to one another as a result through this humorous relationship-strengthening devotional.

Marriage Counseling

To find a reputable marriage counselor, visit http://www.focus onthefamily.com/counseling/find-a-counselor.aspx. Enter your location and the area in which you need counseling. You will be directed to nearby Christian counselors. If you live in Missouri, we recommend Diakonos Counseling (diakonoscounseling.com). Military One Source (www.militaryonesource.com), a Department of Defense organization, will pay for twelve counseling sessions confidentially—nothing will be added to your military record.

Marriage Retreats

Operation Heal Our Patriots (www.operationhealourpatriots .org) is a project of Samaritan's Purse, and it focuses on bringing spiritual refreshment, physical renewal, and marriage enrichment to wounded and injured US military service members and their spouses. To thank these brave men and women for their service and sacrifice, they offer programs uniquely developed to strengthen the marriage relationship and build hope for the future through the transforming power of God's Word.

Helping Children during Deployments

- **Military Kids Connect** (militarykidsconnect.com) is an online community of military children (ages 6–17) that provides access to age-appropriate resources to support children from pre-deployment through a parent's or caregiver's return.

- **Deployment Kids** (deploymentkids.com) is a fun, interactive page for kids that teaches about the country, terrain, and weather conditions of where their parent is deployed. Features include a distance calculator, "I'm proud of you" greeting cards (to download and send to their parent), journaling prompts that allow kids to express their emotions, and much more.

- **United Through Reading Military Program** (www.united throughreading.org/military-program) helps ease the stress of separation for military families by having deployed parents read children's books aloud via DVD for their child to watch at home.

Esteem-Building Resources for Parents of Teens and Preteens

- *Choose to Dance: A Mother/Daughter Guidebook for Tackling Life's Tough Issues* by Penny Monetti. Capture those fleeting moments with your daughter, granddaughter, or special princess in your life with this interactive, humorous, relationship-strengthening resource. Creative dates, introspective ice-breaking questions, and biblical truths are weaved together to lay the foundation to openly discuss challenging topics and uniquely bond relationships.

- *Raising a Modern-Day Knight*: *A Father's Role in Guiding His Son to Authentic Manhood* by Robert Lewis. This book will show how you can confidently guide your son to the kind of authentic, biblical manhood that can change the world.
- *Raising a Modern-Day Princess* by Pam Farrel and Doreen Hanna. This book is designed to equip parents to cultivate strong relationships with their adolescents and stresses the importance of raising a generation of women to see themselves as God sees them—as daughters of the King.

Faith-Growing Opportunities for Kids

- **Eagle Lake** (www.eaglelakecamps.com) was established by the Navigators, an international, interdenominational Christian ministry. This program offers trusted, affordable, and fun Colorado summer camps for kids ages 7–18. With a Christ-centered focus, campers get quality counselor attention and top-notch programs.
- **Kanakuk Christian Sports Kamp** (www.kanakuk.com) focuses on developing dynamic Christian leaders through life-changing experiences, godly relationships, and spiritual training by a Christian staff. Kampers enjoy a program that couples high counselor/Kamper ratios with over seventy sports and activities designed to provide the summer adventure of a lifetime!

- Since 1954, **Fellowship of Christian Athletes** (www.fca .org) has been challenging coaches and athletes on the professional, college, high school, junior high, and youth levels to use the powerful medium of athletics to impact the world for Jesus Christ.
- **K-Life** (www.klife.com) is a youth ministry focused on mentoring, coaching, and disciplining teenagers. K-Life works on a community-wide scale, networking kids from different churches and kids without a church affiliation. Their model of ministry uses evangelism, discipleship, and fellowship to minister to middle school, junior high, and high school students, as well as their families.
- **Military Community Youth Ministries** (www.mcym.org) staff and volunteers seek to love teens unconditionally and provide a model of Christian hope in our military communities through weekly club and fun activities.

Deployment

- **Operation We Are Here** (www.operationwearehere.com) lends support to family members and friends with a deployed loved one. It's also a great resource for finding ideas to encourage a church member, coworker, family member, or friend who is enduring the hardship of a deployed spouse.

Relocating

- **Militarytownadvisor.com** is a wonderful PCS relocation source comprised from military family's reviews regarding neighborhoods, school districts, area businesses, etc. This site was created by a military spouse specifically for military families.

- **Operation Military Family (OMF)** is committed to providing resources to help veterans, active service members, and their families navigate life's transitions. VAPP is one of OMF's flagship tools developed specifically to fast-track connecting veterans and their families to critical services and benefits.

Reintegration

- *Dear God, He's Home!* by Janet Thompson is a practical, honest look at how women can deal with a spouse—regardless of the reason—who is forced to become a stay-at-home man. The unique combination of stresses can take a toll on a marriage.

Transitioning into a New Career

- **Hire Heroes USA** (www.hireherosusa.org) is dedicated to creating job opportunities for US military veterans and their spouses through personalized employment training and corporate engagement.

- **Joining Forces Mentoring Plus** (www.joiningforcesmentoringplus.org) provides resources—including mentors, subject matter experts, and online connections—to women veterans and military and veteran spouses to help them obtain meaningful employment and a successful career.

- **Military One Source** (www.militaryonesource.mil) provides numerous career resources. Go to the website, click "Spouse Education," and then "Career Opportunities."

- **The Military Spouse Career Advancement Accounts** (www.aiportal.acc.af.mil/mycaa/) provides up to four thousand dollars of financial assistance to eligible military spouses who are pursuing a license, certification, or Associate's degree in a portable career field and occupation.

- **Militaryspouse.org** (www.milspouse.org) is a great resource site for spouses to research military scholarships, employment, benefits, and more.

- **National Military Family Association** (www.military family.org) is an organization with strong grassroots support balanced with professionalism. They speak up on behalf of military families and empower husbands, wives, and children to understand and access their benefits.

- **SCORE** (www.score.org) is a nonprofit association dedicated to helping small businesses get off the ground, grow, and achieve their goals through education and mentorship.

- **Transitional Assistance Online** (wwwtaonline.com) is a large source of transition assistance information, jobs, and tools for today's separating military.

- **University of Central Missouri** (ucmo.edu/gateway/focus .cfm). Click on "Focus." Start a free account within minutes, and get ready! Numerous assessments will link you to compatible career choices where you can explore professions, salaries, skill and education requirements, and much more.

- **O Net Online** (onetonline.org) lets you see how your military skills transfer into civilian careers. Once at the site, click "Crosswalks," and then "Military." This resource transfers military skills into compatible civilian careers based on your military occupation specialty (MOS).

- **USAA.com**. After your arrive at the site, click on the "Your Life Events" tab, then "Military," and then "Leaving the Military."

Financial Planning

- *The 5 Money Personalities: Speaking the Same Money and Love Language* by Scott and Bethany Palmer. Every couple argues about money. Scott and Bethany Palmer, aka "The Money Couple," have identified and defined this problem and offer concrete solutions to fix it.
- **Financial Peace** by Dave Ramsey (www.daveramsey.com) is a biblically based curriculum that teaches people how to handle money God's ways.
- **USAA** (www.usaa.com) is a financial institution dedicated to serving our military and veterans and their families. Twenty-five army officers created USAA in 1922. We have no stock in this company, but Tony and I and have been customers for twenty-five years and have never been steered wrong. Take time to visit this invaluable website, even if you have no intentions of doing business. Their financial military deployment site is second to none. Click the "Advice Center" tab, look under the "Military Life" heading, and click "Deployment." Here you'll find resources for deploying service members to use before, during, and after deployments to ensure successful financial management. The site also assists spouses and families during relocations and when separating from the military.

NOTE TO THE READER

The publisher invites you to share your response to the message of this book by writing Discovery House Publishers, P.O. Box 3566, Grand Rapids, MI 49501, U.S.A. For information about other Discovery House books, music, videos, or DVDs, contact us at the same address or call 1-800-653-8333. Find us on the Internet at www.dhp.org or send e-mail to books@dhp.org.

Lieutenant Colonel Tony Monetti is a retired B-2 stealth bomber pilot and the assistant dean of aviation at the University of Central Missouri. He's also the executive director of Skyhaven Airport and the COO of Dodson International Air, a cargo/mission/disaster relief airline. Tony is an Air Force Academy graduate and a combat veteran command pilot of the B-2, B-52, and B-1. His honors include the Distinguished Flying Cross and the Defense Meritorious Service Medal. The Discovery Channel, CNN, and MSNBC news featured his adventurous career as well as two military books: *B-2 Spirit in Action* and *Boeing B-52: Stratofortress Units in Desert Storm*.

Tony is a motivational speaker who inspires groups and top corporate organizations worldwide. His articles have appeared in several military publications such as *Flying Safety*, NATO's *Polaris Quarterly* journal, and *Combat Edge*. Tony was honored as Warrensburg, Missouri's "2010 Man of the Year" for his outstanding contributions to the community.

Penny Monetti is a dynamic, humorous, and poignant speaker who offers family-strengthening presentations to military spouses and organizations nationwide regarding transitions, PTSD care, reintegrations, and battle-proofing military relationships. Penny is certified to help trauma and crisis victims—specifically combat veterans and their families dealing with post-traumatic stress disorder through the American Academy of Christian Counselors and the American Counseling Association. She has been Whiteman Air Force Base's "Joan Orr Spouse of the Year" award winner. She is a member of the military advisory board and represents the voice of the military family for Missouri Congresswoman Vicky Hartzler, who serves on the House Armed Services Committee. Penny uses her experience as an inspirational speaker, military liaison, Air Force wife, and army mom to help military families overcome life's challenges and live life to its fullest.

Together, Tony and Penny have authored *Called to Serve* and *Honored to Serve*. Penny has also authored *Choose to Dance: A Mother/Daughter Guidebook for Tackling Life's Tough Issues* and is a co-contributor to *The Military Wife's New Testament with Psalms and*

Proverbs. Tony and Penny have been guests on radio and television talk shows worldwide, including *Focus on the Family*.

As community leaders, Tony and Penny founded Big Brothers Big Sisters (BBBS) of Johnson County and Connected Hearts, an agency that assists needy and homeless children. Their biggest achievement is raising three beautiful children—still in progress. Their passion is to encourage military families, and they are honored to share their experiences drawn from the military life they have lived and loved for twenty-five years.

If you are interested in having Tony and/or Penny speak at your next engagement, contact them at www.calledtoserveministry.com.

Also by Tony and Penny Monetti

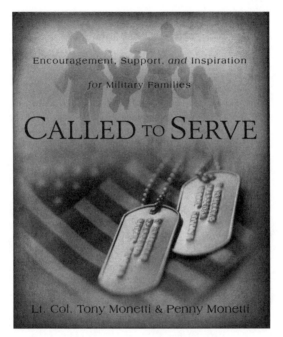

Available wherever books are sold.

To order online, visit www.dhp.org